PFP0099353

CAN WE GET BACK TO FULL EMPLOYMENT?

Maurice Scott
with
Robert A. Laslett

HOLMES & MEIER PUBLISHERS, INC.
New York

First published in the United States of America 1979 by
HOLMES & MEIER PUBLISHERS, INC.
30 Irving Place, New York, N.Y. 10033

Library of Congress Cataloguing in Publication Data

Scott Maurice FitzGerald
  Can we get back to full employment?

Based on the authors' papers which were prepared
for a seminar held at Nuffield College, Nov. 25-26,
1977.
  Bibliography: p.
  Includes index.
  1. Great Britain--Full employment policies.
2. Unemployed--Great Britain. I. Laslett,
Robert A., joint author, II. Title.
HC256.6.S37 1978   331.1'37941   78-10635
ISBN 0-8419-0451-0

PRINTED IN GREAT BRITAIN

ERRATA

The Library of Congress ISBN number given on this page and on the dust
jacket is incorrect. The correct number for this book is 0-8419-0460-X.

The address given for Holmes & Meier Publishers on this page is incorrect. The correct address is IUB Building, 30 Irving Place, New York,
N.Y. 10003.

Contents

List of tables

List of figures

Preface

This book has grown out of two papers which Robert Laslett and myself prepared for a seminar held at Nuffield College on 25th and 26th November 1977. The seminar was the first of a series intended to discuss important policy issues. The idea of holding them originated with A. H. Halsey and Sir Claus Moser, and the topic for this seminar was suggested by Sam Brittan. Both Robert Laslett and myself are grateful to them, and also to the Warden of Nuffield, Sir Norman Chester, who chaired the proceedings, and to all those who attended the seminar and contributed many critical and constructive comments. In particular, we wish to thank those who opened the discussions: Sam Brittan, Jim Durcan, Lord McCarthy and Sir Donald MacDougall. I owe a special debt of gratitude to Sir Donald, who taught me most of the economics I ever knew, and whose own article on 'Inflation in the United Kingdom' said most of what needed to be said nearly 20 years ago. John Flemming's comments and suggestions were also very valuable, not least for Robert Laslett's chapter. The analysis and conclusions which follow have benefited greatly from all of these, as well as from some others who did not attend the seminar. The authors alone remain responsible for the mistakes made and for the views expressed.

M.FG.S.
28th April, 1978

Acknowledgement

Figures 2.1, 2.2 and 5.1 are taken from an article summarising the Report of a Working Party set up by the Department of Employment to study the changed relationship between unemployment and vacancies which appeared in the Department of Employment Gazette, October, 1976. The permission of the Controller of Her Majesty's Stationery Office to reproduce these is gratefully acknowledged.

1 Introduction and Summary

... Mr. Callaghan showed himself much concerned about the high level of unemployment. He said: "What is the cause? Quite simply and unequivocally, it is caused by paying ourselves more than the value of what we produce. There are no scapegoats. This is as true under democratic socialism as it is under capitalism or communism. It is an absolute fact of life which neither the left nor the right can alter."

It used to be thought that a nation could just spend its way out of recession and increase employment by cutting taxes and boosting government spending. "I tell you in all candour that that option no longer exists". In so far as it existed in the past, it had always led to a bigger dose of inflation followed by a higher level of unemployment.

(From a report of the Prime Minister's speech to the Labour Party Conference which appeared in *The Times* (29 September 1976) p. 1)

We have come a long way from the years of full employment which followed the Second World War. In the 19 years 1948–66 registered unemployment averaged 1.7 per cent of the labour force, the highest figure for any year being 2.4 per cent in 1963. Since 1968 unemployment has always been above that highest figure, and in 1977 it averaged 6.3 per cent. In addition, there were many workers whose jobs depended on special state subsidies and there were unemployed persons who did not register. In this book we try to answer the questions: what went wrong? What can be done about it? Can we get back to full employment?

We adopt a simple definition of full employment—it is what we achieved in 1948–66. However, a rather higher unemployment percentage now would be needed to reproduce the same underlying ease or difficulty of securing a job, partly because unemployment benefits have risen in relation to the net-of-tax earnings of those concerned, and partly because of changes in the composition of the labour force and in registration habits. All this is discussed in Chapter 10, by Robert Laslett, who reaches the conclusion that something like 2.7 per cent registered unemployment now would correspond to the 1.7 per cent average of 1948–66. There are many uncertainties in this estimate, but the main point is that it is well below current levels of unemployment.

What, then, explains the rest of the increase? In Chapter 2 we look for proximate causes, and for this purpose it is useful to divide the increase into three parts. There is, first, the increase in *frictional* unemployment, that is, in the unemployment which would still exist even at the top of a boom, and even when the structure of the labour force was as well adapted to the structure of demand for labour as in the full employment era. The reasons why frictional unemployment has increased are those just mentioned, and discussed in Chapter 10. Secondly, there is the increase in *cyclical* unemployment, due to the fall in demand in what has been the worst slump since the 1930s. Finally, there is the remaining increase in unemployment, which we call *structural*. The evidence that there has been an increase which is greater than can be explained by the factors already mentioned relates mainly to the boom of 1973. In that year, despite the fact that other indicators suggest that the pressure of demand was as high as in the strongest boom of the full employment era, 1955, unemployment amounted to 2.7 per cent, compared with 1.1 per cent in 1955. The rise in frictional unemployment can only explain part of this difference, leaving the rest to be explained by structural factors—which, we think, have operated to increase unemployment still further since then. Our examination of the employment statistics in Chapter 2 turns up another notable development. At least until 1974, the fall in employment and growth in unemployment was almost entirely confined to males, while female employment continued to grow. The relation of this to the growth in structural unemployment is considered in Chapter 5.

After reviewing these proximate causes of the increase in unemployment, we turn to the more fundamental causes. In Chapter 3 we consider the level of demand. High demand was achieved in 1948–66 mainly as the result of a prolonged investment boom, together with rapid growth in world trade. Subsequently, the recession of recent years was due mainly to a rise in private savings and a worsening in our terms of trade, following the oil and commodity price increases in 1972–3, which reduced purchasing power. Investment fell in relation to trend, but not by very much, and there were various factors which had sizeable effects on exports or imports but which, taken together, roughly cancelled each other out. One interesting point emerging from this analysis is that budget deficits did not boost demand in the full employment era, instead, there were budget surpluses to restrain it. In the recent recession, budget deficits have countered some of the fall in demand—but not very much of it.

All this does not take us very far in explaining either why we had full-employment in 1948–66, or why we have lost it since. How was it that we were able to *permit* such a high level of demand in the earlier period without running into inflationary problems to any great extent? Why, given the post-war commitment to full employment, did we not do more to counteract the recent recession? Furthermore, why has unemployment increased in recent years for reasons apparently unconnected with deficient demand (structural unemployment)?

The main reason why demand was not maintained at a higher level in recent years was the breakdown of wage restraint. The original architects of full employment policy, and the successive governments which operated it, were all worried by this possibility, as is pointed out in Chapter 4. Their 'toothless jawboning' on the subject may have helped to delay the breakdown, but the main reasons for this delay probably lay elsewhere. First, workers' 'militancy' had taken some severe knocks between the wars, and so they reacted cautiously to the new conditions. Gradually, however, the older workers gave way to younger ones for whom full employment was the normal state of affairs. The student riots in Paris in 1968 (themselves preceded by riots in the U.S.A., perhaps due to dissatisfaction with conscription for the Vietnam war) may have sparked the wage explosion of 1969–70. There was a dramatic increase in the number of working days lost through strikes. We call those who subscribe to this type of theory *'militants'* for short. Secondly, price expectations were very slow to adjust to the reality of post-war inflation, but, when they did, this led to much larger wage and price increases than before. *Monetarists* would presumably emphasise this type of explanation. A third possible explanation is provided by those who believe that workers set themselves a target to hit, this being a rate of increase in real disposable wages. Real wages rose much faster after the war than during the inter-war years. However, the increasing share of public expenditure and rising tax rates meant that real disposable wages rose rather slowly after 1966, and this is the explanation for wage pressure favoured by target theorists, or '*marksmen*' as we shall call them for short. We review the different ways in which militants, monetarists, and marksmen explain what determines wage changes, and try to synthesise their views, as would a '*mixer*'.

The main reason why 'structural' unemployment grew was that more investment became labour-saving rather than labour-using. We argue in Chapter 5 that, *cet. par.*, an increase in the share of wages in value-added will have two effects on investment: it will tend to reduce its total amount, and it will increase the share of labour-saving investment. We contrast the records of manufacturing industry and of the main private service industries excluding distribution. Whereas the share of wages rose strongly in manufacturing value-added, it changed little in services. Employment fell in manufacturing after 1966, whereas it rose in services. The ratio of investment to value-added did not, in the event, fall in manufacturing until quite recently—tax concessions and other factors may have helped to maintain it. In services, the same ratio rose strongly.

Our argument is, then, that the slowing down in the growth of capacity and output in manufacturing after 1966, and the accompanying fall in manufacturing employment, was mainly due to a switch from capacity-increasing and labour-using investment to labour-saving investment which created little new capacity and probably even destroyed some. This slower growth in capacity explains why the 1973 boom in demand hit the ceiling of capacity so soon, even though unemployment still was high. It was not because (as is sometimes supposed) output expanded unusually fast, for it did not. Some people have objected to this hypothesis that there is no evidence of any change in the relationship between output and employment such as they would expect to result from a switch from labour-using to labour-saving investment. However, as we point out, there is no reason to expect a change of that kind, so that the objection is groundless.

Why did manufacturing fare so much worse than private services? The main reason probably was the government's exchange rate and other macroeconomic policies. Manufacturing, producing tradeable goods, found its profits squeezed by foreign competition, both at home and abroad, whereas services were better able to maintain or increase profit margins. However, the fact that it was mainly the industries employing *males* that suffered, whereas those employing many *females* continued to expand, may have had some relevance to the outcome. Female employees were cheaper, and may, for one reason or another, have become 'better buys' over this period. This is an interesting hypothesis, but we can explain by far the greater part of the difference between the male and female employment record in terms of structural shifts in the economy due to the factors already mentioned, and some others, notably, the rapid growth in employment in education, health and other public services. To explain the most striking change of all, the decline in manufacturing employment after 1966, we come back to the same fundamental factor as before. The government *could* have operated with a more devalued exchange rate and a more expansionary policy, with a lower share of wages in value-added. It chose not to because it feared the inflationary consequences.

The conclusion to which Chapters 4 and 5 both point is the same. Both cyclical and structural unemployment were allowed to increase because lower unemployment and a larger share of profits would have resulted in even more inflation than we had to suffer as it was. As Mr. Callaghan put it succinctly in the quotation at the beginning of this chapter, we have paid ourselves too much and that has been the main cause of rising unemployment. We do not accept the view, still widely prevalent, that it was weakness in our balance of payments which forced us to let unemployment increase. There *was* a balance of payments constraint throughout most of the full employment era, when we had a fixed exchange rate with the dollar; but, looking back now, we can see that it was never very severe. The abandonment of the fixed exchange rate means that inflation rather than the balance of payments is now the real constraint. It is thus misleading to attribute our difficulties in some way to foreign trade: without it, or with less of it, it would in fact be harder to get back to full employment. All this is discussed in Chapter 6.

In Chapter 7 we list, and briefly review, in the light of militant, monetarist and marksmen theories, a number of policies which have been suggested to deal with the problem: (a) raising aggregate demand together with depreciation of the exchange rate as required, (b) the same, but with import restrictions replacing depreciation of the exchange rate, (c) increasing the rate of growth of real disposable wages, (d) increasing the rate of growth of employment in public services and/or reducing the rate of growth of the total labour force, (e) incomes policy, (f) monetarist policies, (g) policies proposed in a recent OECD Report, (h) policies proposed in a recent CBI Report, (i) various more radical policies proposed by Messrs. Meade, Brittan and Jay. As the discussion in Chapter 7 *is* brief we make no attempt to summarise it here.

Chapter 8 is addressed mainly to economists. The ideas and arguments of the preceding chapters are brought together, and their interrelationships explored, with the help of a diagrammatic model of the economy. We consider both the full-employment era and the years of rising unemployment and inflation which followed it. We also analyse the long-term effects of the different policies considered in Chapter 7.

Most of this book is an attempt to clarify thought about the problem of securing full employment. We look at the historical record, and we consider different hypotheses. It is impossible to either prove or refute altogether any of the hypotheses by an appeal to the record—history is too complicated for that. Nevertheless, decisions must somehow be taken and policies formulated, and so a judgement has to be reached on what are the main changes needed if we are to get back to full employment. The writer's view, for what it is worth, is that no measures will be successful unless they include some reform of our present system for fixing wages. This conclusion is briefly expounded in Chapter 9.

2 What is full employment?

From 1948 to 1966 inclusive total registered unemployment in the U.K. (excluding those temporarily stopped but including students and school leavers) averaged 1.7 per cent of the number of employees, the highest percentage for any year being 2.4 (in 1963), and the lowest 1.1 (in 1955) (see Table 2.1). In 1967 the percentage rose to 2.3 and has never fallen below it since. In 1977 it was 6.3 per cent. 'Getting back to full employment' could be interpreted, quite simply, as getting the unemployment percentage back to the average levels achieved from 1948 to 1966.

Commonsense and the statistics both suggest, however, that registered unemployment increases if unemployment benefits are raised in relation to earnings at work net of tax, as has happened in the U.K. as well as in some other countries. Registered unemployment will also increase if people who used not to register when they were unemployed now do so. Examples in the U.K. are students, part-time workers and some married women. Some part of the increase in unemployment since 1966 is due to these factors, and so it would seem to be right to regard a rather higher percentage now as being the equivalent, in some sense, of the 1.7 per cent achieved from 1948 to 1966. 'Equivalent', that is, in regard to the pressure of demand for labour, or the ease with which unemployed labour can find a job, or an employer can find workers. Just how much higher an equivalent percentage would be is hard to judge. This whole question is discussed in chapter 10 by Robert Laslett, and the conclusion reached there is that 2.7 per cent unemployment now would be roughly equivalent, in the above sense,

TABLE 2.1

Annual Percentage Changes in Income from Employment per Employee in Employment and in the Retail Price Index; and the Level of Unemployment 1948–77

	Income from Employment		Retail Price Index (3)	% Unemployment in earlier year (4)
	Nominal (1)	Real (2)		
1948–49	7.0	4.2	2.8	1.6
49–50	4.6	1.7	2.7	1.6
50–51	9.5	0.0	9.5	1.6
51–52	7.7	−0.8	8.7	1.3
52–53	5.0	1.7	3.2	1.8
53–54	5.0	3.1	1.8	1.7
54–55	8.2	3.5	4.6	1.4
55–56	8.1	2.9	4.9	1.1
56–57	5.8	2.1	3.7	1.2
57–58	5.0	1.9	3.0	1.5
58–59	3.9	3.3	0.6	2.1
59–60	5.4	4.3	1.1	2.2
60–61	6.9	3.6	3.3	1.7
61–62	5.0	0.6	4.3	1.5
62–63	4.9	2.9	1.9	2.0
63–64	7.1	3.1	3.9	2.4
64–65	6.8	2.0	4.6	1.7
65–66	6.3	2.5	3.7	1.5
66–67	6.1	3.6	2.4	1.5
67–68	7.8	2.9	4.8	2.3
68–69	7.1	1.9	5.2	2.5
69–70	12.9	5.9	6.5	2.5
70–71	11.8	2.1	9.5	2.6
71–72	12.3	5.1	6.8	3.4
72–73	12.5	3.8	8.4	3.8
73–74	20.7	4.0	15.9	2.7
74–75	30.9	5.3	24.2	2.7
75–76	14.8	−0.8	15.8	4.3
76–77	8.8	−6.3	16.0	5.9
77–78	n.a.	n.a.	n.a.	6.3

NOTE: The series in Cols. (1) and (2) were obtained by calculating percentage changes in original series given to one place of decimals with 1970 = 100. They are therefore subject to rounding errors.

SOURCES:

(1) 1954–77 *National Institute Economic Review*, linking series there given. 1948–54 linked on using *National Income and Expenditure 1959* and *British Labour Statistics Historical Abstract 1886–1968.*

(2) Series in Col. (1) deflated by that in Col. (3).
(3) *National Institute Economic Review*, linking series there given. From 1974 on the series are stated to exclude seasonal foods, but it is not thought that this significantly affects the annual average.
(4) Total registered unemployment in the U.K. (annual average of monthly figures), excuding temporarily stopped but including school leavers and adult students, as a percentage of mid-year numbers of employees in civil employment plus annual average unemployment. 1948-61, *British Labour Statistics Historical Abstract 1886-68*; 1962-72, *Annual Abstract of Statistics 1973*; 1973-77, *Dept. of Employment Gazette*.

to 1.7 per cent then. In what follows, we adopt this definition of 'full employment', although the exact percentage is not crucial to the argument. The important point is that it is much below the current figure of over 6 per cent.

Our fundamental definition of full employment thus refers to the ease or difficulty of getting jobs (for workers) or workers (for employers), and we measure this by reference to the statistics of registered unemployment. We realise that these statistics are not an ideal measure. We examine its relationship to another possible measure, the number of vacancies notified to employment exchanges (or job centres as they are now called), below. We also realise that there is a great deal of unregistered unemployment, and also of employment which exists by virtue of special subsidies from the government. In January, 1978, the Secretary of State for Employment stated that the special employment measures operated by his department (the temporary employment subsidy, the small firms employment subsidy and the job release scheme) were assisting 310,000 workers, or about 1.4 per cent of the labour force. Many more are employed as a result of subsidies to British Leyland, British Steel and the large sums disbursed as regional grants to industry. It is also true that overmanning exists in various industries, both private and public, the extent of which was vividly revealed by the remarkably small drop in output which accompanied the three day working week in 1974. However, this book is not about efficiency in British industry, nor the extent to which output could be increased with the existing labour force if it were better used. We are trying to answer a different question, namely, can we get back to the situation which ruled in the labour market in this country for about 20 years after the Second World War?

THREE PROXIMATE REASONS FOR THE
INCREASE IN UNEMPLOYMENT

Taking our measure of registered unemployment, we need, then, to explain why it has increased from the average of 1.7 per cent in 1948–66 to 6.3 per cent in 1977, and then to consider ways in which it could be reduced. In this chapter we confine attention to the proximate reasons for the increase, and for this purpose it is useful to distinguish three which we label *frictional, cyclical* and *structural.* We shall use these labels as if they referred to different kinds of unemployment, since this is commonly done. However, it is as well to be clear that we are really discussing reasons for changes in the level of unemployment. In general, we cannot point to unemployed persons and meaningfully say 'You are frictionally unemployed, whereas you, sir, are cyclically unemployed, and you, madam, are structurally unemployed'. This would seldom make sense. It does make sense, however, to divide the total increase in unemployment since the full-employment era into these three categories, as we shall shortly do. Let us first consider what they mean.

(a) *Frictional unemployment*

At the top of a boom there will still be some unemployed persons. In 1955, for example, there were 1.1 per cent, which is the lowest percentage achieved in any year since the war (see Table 2.1). This unemployment existed because there are always some people who have just left one job and have not yet found another, or some school-leavers or students who have not yet found their first job, and there are also some people for whom it is very difficult to find suitable work because, for example, they are handicapped, or because they are not very eager to work. During the war, it proved possible to reduce unemployment to even lower levels, but we may reasonably regard 1.1 per cent as about the minimum possible level in the freer economy of peacetime. We call this 'irreducible minimum' *frictional unemployment.* Its level can, in fact, change, as we shall presently see. However, its meaning is the amount of unemployment remaining at the top of a strong boom (as strong as in 1955) and in a period in which the labour force is as well adjusted to the structure of production as in the full employment era of 1948–66. By definition, then, in 1955 there was only frictional unemployment, and cyclical and structural unemployment were both zero.

(b) *Cyclical unemployment*

Unemployment fluctuated in the full employment era between the low of 1.1 per cent just mentioned and a high of 2.4 per cent in 1963. The average was 1.7 per cent. If we can assume that the labour force remained as well adapted to the structure of production as in 1955 throughout this period, as seems reasonable, then we can say that cyclical unemployment averaged 0.6 per cent over this period, varying between zero in 1955 and 1.3 per cent in 1963. It is thus defined as the excess of actual unemployment over frictional unemployment in a period when there is no structural unemployment. Alternatively, if there is structural unemployment, we can still estimate cyclical unemployment provided the former is constant. For then cyclical unemployment will be the excess of actual unemployment over its level at the top of a strong boom.

(c) *Structural unemployment*

Finally, we need to define *structural unemployment*. The main idea, that it is due to a mismatch between the available labour force and the productive structure, was stated above. The mismatch may be due to regional factors (too much labour in the North or West and not enough in the Midlands or the South East), to skill factors (too many unskilled workers and not enough skilled ones), or to the rapidity with which the pattern of output is changing (although this could perhaps better be regarded as a factor tending to increase frictional unemployment). It might also be due to demographic factors. Since women and young persons tend to experience higher rates of labour turnover, an increasing proportion of these groups in the work force could increase the level of unemployment (but, again, one might better classify this as an increase in frictional unemployment). The factor to which we shall attribute most importance is, however, rather different from these. It is an insufficiency of labour-using investment, that is, of investment which increases the demand for labour. Labour-saving investment tends to change the structure of production in such a way as to reduce employment. Unless it is balanced by sufficient labour-using investment, then, employment will fall and structural unemployment will increase. From what has been said, it should be clear that the best way to see whether structural unemployment has increased is to compare years at the same stage in the business cycle: two years at the top of the boom, for example. If, after allowing for changes in frictional unemployment, there remains some increase in total unemployment, then that can be attributed to structural factors.

THE INCREASE IN UNEMPLOYMENT SINCE 1966

As was mentioned at the beginning of this chapter, there has almost certainly been an increase in frictional unemployment since 1966. Robert Laslett's examination of various surveys which have been made of the unemployed suggests that in 1973, the most recent boom year, there was an increase in unemployment, compared with the pre-1966 situation, of about 0.6 per cent which could be attributed to such factors as increases in earnings related unemployment benefits and increases in the numbers of part-time workers registering as unemployed. If all of this represented an increase in frictional unemployment, then we could put its level at 1.7 per cent in 1973. However, this may be too high, for reasons given below.

The actual level of unemployment in 1973 was 2.7 per cent. What then accounted for the difference between this figure and the frictional element, a difference of at least 1 per cent? It seems unlikely that any appreciable part of it was due to cyclical factors, since 1973 was a boom year. Indeed, to judge by the number of unfilled vacancies notified to employment exchanges, the pressure of demand on firms' capacity was as strong as in 1955. This can be seen from two very interesting figures which are reproduced from the Department of Employment Gazette for October 1976. Figure 2.1 relates to male and Figure 2.2 to female vacancies and unemployment.

From Fig. 2.1, it can be seen that from 1952 to 1966 male unemployment and vacancies behaved in a consistent way. In boom years, such as 1955 or 1965, unemployment was low and vacancies were high. In slump years, such as 1958 and 1963, unemployment was (relatively) high and vacancies were low. All the observations therefore more or less lie along a (curved) line at the left-hand side of the figure. The relationship illustrated by this line is well-known, an early analysis of it being that of Dow and Dicks-Mireaux (Feb. 1958). After 1966, however, this stable relationship disappeared. Unemployment increased without vacancies falling very much. By 1972, male unemployment was close to 700,000 with vacancies higher than

FIG. 2.1 *Male unemployment and vacancies*[1] *(Great Britain, 1952–75) June figures*[2] *shown*

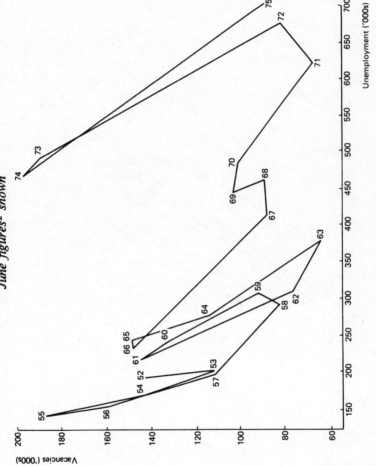

[1] Vacancies are those suitable for adults (since April 1974, those notified to Employment Offices)
[2] All figures are seasonally adjusted, in thousands

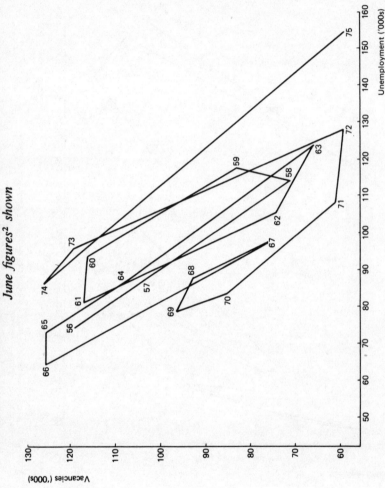

FIG. 2.2   *Female unemployment and vacancies[1] (Great Britain 1956–75)*
June figures[2] shown

[1]Vacancies are those suitable for adults (since April 1974, those notified to Employment Offices
[2]All figures are seasonally adjusted, in thousands

in 1962 or 1963, and about the same as in 1958, when unemployment was around 300,000 less. Then, in 1973 (and 1974), when demand expanded, vacancies increased sharply and unemployment fell, but the new curve was much further to the right than before. What factor or factors can explain its shift to the right, implying an increase of around 300,000 to 350,000 unemployed or about 1.4 per cent of the labour force for a given level of vacancies? Laslett's figures suggest that at most only about a half of this increase can be attributed to an increase in frictional unemployment, leaving the rest to be explained by an increase in structural unemployment.

Two further points should be noted. First, the figure shows no year later than 1975. From mid-1975 to mid-1977 male unemployment increased from around 700,000 to nearly 1,000,000. Total vacancies (male and female—separate figures are no longer collected) changed little, and so one might conclude that there has been a further increase of about 300,000 in male unemployment due to other than cyclical factors since 1975. However, this probably exaggerates the importance of these other factors. As Fig. 2.1 suggests, there is a minimum level of unfilled vacancies due to inevitable 'frictions' in the labour market, and present levels of vacancies may be close to that minimum. Hence some of the further increase of 300,000 in male unemployment since 1975 was probably due to cyclical factors. Nevertheless, it would probably be wrong to regard *all* of it as being due to that cause. We may therefore tentatively conclude that structural unemployment has increased further since then.

The second point to note is that *female* unemployment did not behave like male unemployment. This is shown in Fig. 2.2. From 1956 until 1974, the relationship between female unemployment and vacancies was reasonably stable. Hence one could plausibly say that here at least most of the variations in unemployment were due to cyclical factors. Between 1966 and 1974, when vacancies were more or less the same, unemployment increased by only some 20,000. Changes in female unemployment between these years therefore explain very little of the increase in total unemployment, male and female. This suggests that the 'other factors' responsible for the increase in unemployment, which we have yet to explain, were in some way or other particularly associated with males, not females. After 1974, however, the picture changes. From 1974 to 1975, as Fig. 2.2 shows, there was obviously a drop in demand for females. Vacancies fell and unemployment rose. Furthermore, the increase in female unemployment was *more* than could have been expected from the fall in vacancies. From mid-1975 to mid -1977 (not shown on the Figure) female unemployment increased by a further 170,000. Hence, since 1974, female unemployment has behaved much more like male unemployment.

We cannot draw any very precise conclusions about the magnitudes of our three different proximate causes of increased unemployment. Nevertheless, it seems reasonable to infer that each of the three was important in 1977. Let us take them in increasing order of importance.

Frictional unemployment may have increased by as much as 0.6 per cent of the labour force in 1973 compared with the full employment era. This is Laslett's estimate of the increase in unemployment in that year due to increased earnings related unemployment benefits and to some other factors already mentioned. His corresponding estimate for 1976 is 1.3 per cent. How should we interpret this increase? One possible interpretation (a pessimistic one) is that attitudes to work are gradually changing as a result of the increased ratio of income received by someone out of work to the income (net of tax) received at work, especially for low paid workers. Laslett's figures show that for many such workers there is little or no financial inducement to work, and it seems likely that this state of affairs must eventually affect attitudes to work. If so, frictional unemployment may have increased from, say, 1.7 per cent in 1973 (i.e. 1.1 as in 1955 plus 0.6) to 2.4 per cent in 1976 (i.e. 1.1 plus 1.3). Since then, it may have increased still further.

But there is a more optimistic interpretation. In 1976 *total* unemployment was more than twice as great as in 1973. Might not some at least of the increase in Laslett's figure be due to this increase in total unemployment? If the effect of greater unemployment benefits in relation to earnings net of tax is to make the unemployed take longer over their search for new jobs, then one would indeed expect this to be the case. Likewise, if more part-time workers are registering as unemployed, the number who register will increase as the boom is followed by a slump. In short, only part of Laslett's figures can be regarded as an increase in frictional unemployment as we have defined it, and the rest is cyclical or structural. Hence frictional unemployment may not have increased even by as much as 0.6 per cent, since there was some structural unemployment in 1973, and some of the 0.6 per cent may have related to that. At this point we will anticipate our discussion in chapter 5 of the factors making for increased structural unemployment to note that there is little evidence of a more varied change in the pattern of employment, nor is it thought that demographic factors have appreciably increased unemployment. Hence it is unlikely that either of these factors, which could as well be regarded as causing frictional as structural unemployment, were very significant. In which case, frictional unemployment in 1977 may have been less than 1.7 per cent, although it could also, as we have seen, have been as high as 2.4 per cent.

Structural unemployment in 1973 increased by at least 1 per cent of the labour force as compared with the full employment era. By 1977 it was almost certainly over 1 per cent, and one could put up a case for the view that it was close to 3 per cent. Thus Figs. 2.1 and 2.2, brought up to 1977, could be interpreted as showing a rightward shift in the unemployment/vacancies relationship of about 800,000 for males and females together since the full employment era. This is 3.4 per cent of the labour force. If one deducts something less than 0.6 per cent for the increase in frictional unemployment one is left with an increase in structural unemployment of close to 3 per cent. However, this exaggerates its importance, since part of the apparent rightward shift in the unemployment/vacancies relationship was very likely due to increasing cyclical unemployment, unaccompanied by any fall in unfilled vacancies because they had reached a minimum. Part may also have been due to a further increase in frictional unemployment.

Finally, *cyclical unemployment* was negligible in 1973, but large in 1977. For example, if we put frictional unemployment then at 1.7 per cent, and structural unemployment also at 1.7 per cent, cyclical unemployment must have been 2.9 per cent.

A return to full employment would mean, first, a reduction in this very high level of cyclical unemployment to something closer to the average of 0.6 per cent achieved from 1948 to 1966. Because of the factors discussed by Laslett, and also possibly because we must now expect larger cycles in output and employment, we may have to accept a higher average than this, perhaps as high as 1.0 per cent. Given time, it should be possible to get rid of structural unemployment altogether—or, to be more precise, to restore it to the levels achieved in 1948 to 1966 which we have implicitly included in our definition of frictional unemployment. Finally, given the present relationship between unemployment benefits and earnings net of tax, frictional unemployment could well increase as people's work habits, and attitudes to work, gradually change. However, it seems unlikely that the present disincentives to work, which, as Laslett shows, are very severe indeed for lower paid workers, will be allowed to persist. It would not, then, be too optimistic to suppose that frictional unemployment could be held at around 1.7 per cent. This rough figuring suggests that full employment on our definition would mean an average level of unemployment of 2.7 per cent, that is, about 1 per cent more than in 1948 to 1966.

We have not, however, discussed the difficulties which lie in the way of achieving that figure. They emerge only too clearly from the following chapters.

3 Aggregate demand

POST-WAR DEMAND COMPARED WITH PRE-WAR

Writing in 1968, Matthews (September 1968) asked 'Why has Britain had full employment since the war?' He pointed out that, in the inter-war period, unemployment (measured on a comparable basis) averaged about $10\frac{1}{2}$ per cent, while before 1914, according to the best (but uncertain) estimates available, it averaged about $4\frac{1}{2}$ per cent. The post-war average of 1.7 per cent was therefore unusually low by historical standards.

Applying a straightforward Keynesian analysis, Matthews concluded that the main explanation for the low level of unemployment was the strength of investment demand, plus (if one made the comparison with the very depressed 1930's rather than the less depressed 1920's) the stronger demand for exports. If one excludes housebuilding, it was private rather than public sector investment which accounted for most of the increase in investment demand, and Matthews suggested several reasons as to why it should have been (historically speaking) so strong. Viewing actual investment as the outcome of a demand curve reflecting the amount of investment opportunities at given rates of return, and of a supply curve, reflecting the willingness of businessmen to invest different amounts at given rates of return, he pointed out that there were factors increasing both demand and supply. On the demand side, there were the sort of factors found in any investment boom: the jacking up of output in the war increased incomes and demand after it; stronger export demand; the accumulation of investment opportunities due to the fact that investment had been sluggish throughout the 20th Century (with two world wars, the Great Depression of the 1930's, the relatively depressed 1920's and the stagnation of 1900–1914); and, possibly, faster technical progress in the post-war world. On the supply side, businessmen could have been encouraged to invest by the government's commitment to full-employment, by cheap money, and by tax concessions. The last certainly became more generous during the post-war period, but interest rates also rose, and Matthews was not sure how the average position compared with pre-war. If supply factors had been important, rates of return should have fallen as compared with pre-war. The higher level of investment would then have been mainly due to businessmen being willing to invest more at any given rate of return, and, in the face of an unchanged demand curve of investment opportunities, this should have driven down the rate of return. Matthews doubted, however, whether rates of return were lower. It then looked as if both demand and supply factors caused an increase in private investment from pre-war to post-war.

One interesting feature of this analysis is that Matthews did not attribute any direct role to Keynesian deficit financing. As he pointed out, the very opposite was true: the government consistently ran a large current account surplus. So far from stimulating demand through budget deficits, the government restricted demand through budget surpluses. Of course, to some extent the surpluses themselves were the *result* of full employment, which both increased tax revenues and reduced expenditure on unemployment benefits. But even allowing for this, Matthews believed that post-war budgets were more restrictive than pre-war ones. It is still possible that the *commitment* to full employment, by increasing business confidence, *indirectly* stimulated private investment.

There are several criticisms which can be made of Matthew's answer to the question 'How did we achieve full employment in the post-war years?' The omission of any discussion of inflation or wage restraint seems, with the benefit of hindsight, surprising. There is no discussion either of labour-saving versus labour-using investment. We return to these points in subsequent chapters.

Even if we confine ourselves to an analysis in terms of aggregate demand, a Keynesian might say that, although strong private investment demand was the *actual* reason why aggregate demand was sufficient to generate full employment, it was not a *necessary condition*.

Given the government's commitment to full employment, if private investment had not increased as compared with before the war, some other component of final demand could have taken its place. Private consumption could have been stimulated by tax cuts, or public consumption or investment could have been increased further. The fact that these additional sources of demand were not needed was evidence, perhaps, of the responsiveness of private investment to high demand. As Matthews said, it is possible that one only had to prime the pump for the water to gush out. Hence, in a more fundamental sense, it was after all the commitment to full employment which really mattered.

THE RECENT RECESSION

Turning to the more recent fall in demand, with its accompanying rise in cyclical unemployment, Taylor (1978) has provided an analysis based on broadly the same method as that of Matthews. He seeks to explain the shortfall of the gross domestic product (GDP) in the recession years of 1975–77 as compared with the level which the GDP would have reached had it continued on the trend established in the years 1963–74. The explanation is, again, in terms of 'exogenous' changes in certain components of demand, of which the two most important deflationary ones are the increase in the private average propensity to save and the worsening in the terms of trade (i.e. higher import prices, relative to export prices, cutting the purchasing power of incomes generated in the U.K.). Each of these is estimated to have reduced demand by about 4 per cent of GDP. Interestingly enough, private investment is thought to have reduced demand by only a further $1\frac{1}{2}$ per cent of GDP so, although it was the most important factor in Matthew's analysis of the increase in demand from pre-war, it has apparently been a rather minor factor in the recent recession. Nevertheless, the analysis does highlight a very disappointing feature of recent experience. Despite the evident desire of the private sector to save more, private investment has fallen below trend. There seems to have been a failure of the system to respond to savers' intentions. We return to this in Chapter 5.

As well as the factors mentioned, whose combined effect is estimated to have caused a fall of about 10 per cent in the GDP below trend, there were some offsetting factors. There was a small net inflationary effect on the volume of exports and imports taken together. Trade liberalisation, for example, increased our exports (an inflationary effect) but it also increased our imports (a deflationary effect). The Government increased its fiscal deficit. The net result was that GDP fell 7 per cent below trend in 1975–77.

This has been, in fact, easily the worst recession since the war, and one naturally asks what has become of the commitment to full employment? The Government may have offset some of the deflationary influences by the Keynesian remedy of a fiscal deficit, but why did it not offset much more?

CONCLUSION

To conclude this chapter, high demand, due mainly to strong private investment demand and also strong demand for exports, helped to maintain full employment from 1948 to 1966. Since then, and especially since 1973–4, demand has weakened and cyclical unemployment has increased. But this does not take us very far in explaining either why we achieved full employment in the earlier period or why we failed to achieve it subsequently. The first question we must ask is why we were able to *permit* such high demand from 1948 to 1966, and not able to maintain it thereafter? There is also a second question: Why did unemployment, especially male unemployment, increase after 1966 for reasons apparently unconnected with deficient demand?

There are two obvious answers to the first question. One is that the government was afraid of the inflationary consequences of reflating demand. In the writer's view this is the fundamental explanation, and so we discuss the causes of inflation in the next chapter. But another answer might be that the government was afraid of the balance of payments consequences of reflating demand. From time to time this has certainly appeared to be the right answer, and its importance has often been emphasised. We therefore discuss it separately in Chapter 6.

To answer the second question, we must provide an explanation for the increase in structural unemployment, and this we attempt to give in Chapter 5.

4 Inflation and wage restraint

The average rate of increase of the retail price index from 1948 to 1966 was only 3.8 per cent per annum. At the time, this seemed quite high, and was indeed so compared with the experience of the preceding centuries, but in retrospect it seems astonishing that unemployment could be on average as low as 1.7 per cent with inflation at such a moderate level and with no sign that it was accelerating.

Those who had advocated the commitment to full employment had certainly been worried that it might lead to inflation. Thus, in a chapter entitled 'General Conditions of a High and Stable Level of Employment' the 1944 White Paper on *Employment Policy* remarked 'Action taken by the Government to maintain expenditure will be fruitless unless wages and prices are kept reasonably stable . . . . If we are to operate with success a policy for maintaining a high and stable level of employment, it will be essential that employers and workers should exercise moderation in wages matters so that increased expenditure provided at the onset of a depression may go to increase the volume of employment'. Beveridge (1944, p. 199) wrote 'Making the labour market generally a seller's market rather than a buyer's market will increase permanently and markedly the bargaining strength of labour . . . . There is a real danger that sectional wage bargaining, pursued without regard to its effects upon prices, may lead to a vicious spiral of inflation, with money wages chasing prices and without any gain in real wages for the working class as a whole . . . . The fact remains that there is no inherent mechanism in our present system, which can with certainty prevent competitive sectional bargaining for wages from setting up a vicious spiral of rising prices under full employment'.

THE EFFECTS OF INCOMES POLICIES

The successive governments which operated the policy were also worried about inflation. In the years up to 1966, several attempts were made to prevent or moderate wage increases and price increases. There was the 1948–50 Cripps price freeze with wage restraint, the 1956 Macmillan 'price plateau', the 1961–2 Selwyn-Lloyd 'pay pause' followed by the 'guiding light' until 1964, and finally the 1964–6 Brown 'statement of intent', followed by a statutory wage and price freeze in 1966. At the time it looked as if none of these was successful for more than a short period, but looking back one has to admit that the whole period was really one of great success. We had never had it so good, and many people would now eagerly accept the combination of full employment, moderate inflation, and moderate (but historically rapid) growth if we could but achieve it again. Why were we able to achieve it then?

Despite the pasting incomes policies have received from many quarters (see especially Brittan and Lilley, 1977), there are reasons for believing that the frequent attempts by governments to moderate wage and price increases probably had *some* effect. As Tobin (March 1972, p. 17) has put it 'guideposts do not wholly deserve the scorn that "toothless jawboning" often attracts. There is an arbitrary, imitative component in wage settlements, and maybe it can be influenced by national standards.'

There is some econometric evidence that incomes policies have slowed down the annual rate of wage increases temporarily, though usually only by one or two percentage points. It is often pointed out that the gains here were wiped out in subsequent wage explosions, so that the long-term effects could have even been the reverse of those intended. However, at the very least this suggests that wage increases *are* susceptible to this kind of influence. Furthermore, we do not know what would have happened if post-war governments had totally ignored the problem. It is possible that accelerating inflation might then have started much sooner than it did. The successive incomes policies may have kept down the norm for wage increases, partly by influencing negotiators' expectations about wage increases which would be conceded elsewhere, and about price increases, and partly by influencing those on both sides whose natural reflex action is to heed the wishes of their elected government.

At all events, when, in the autumn of 1969, the government abandoned all attempts to restrain wages, they started to accelerate upwards quite rapidly, despite growing slack in the economy, gently rising unemployment, and a tendency for consumer prices to accelerate later and more slowly. Much the same, only on a far greater scale, happened after the General Election in February 1974, when the incoming (Labour) government abandoned the outgoing (Conservative) one's income policy and replaced it by what was, in effect, a free-for-all. Wages accelerated much faster than in 1969, despite a deepening recession, faster increasing unemployment, and consumer price increases which, although much faster than in 1969, yet lagged well behind wage increases. Admittedly each of these episodes could be blamed on the anomalies created by preceding incomes policies, by the determination to get in your wage increase before the next round of incomes policy and, in the second episode, by the cost-of-living thresholds. Nevertheless, both episodes are difficult to reconcile with the simple view that wage increases are totally uninfluenced by "toothless jawboning" or its absence.

The writer would not, however, place most emphasis on government policy as the restraining factor on wage increases from 1948 to 1966. Two other influences were probably more important: the cautious behaviour of trade union members and leaders, whose memories of the inter-war years were still fresh; and the long history of price stability before the war. We consider these in turn.

INCREASING MILITANCY

Brown (March 1975, p. 4) has pointed out the similarities (not just in the U.K. but in many other countries as well) between the 1970's and the years before 1914. 'The developments of recent years have confronted many observers with a prospect of social disruption. People have come to fear that the country is ungovernable, that it is bent on tearing itself to pieces. Forces have asserted themselves that established procedures cannot contain. Yet so it was too, sixty and more years ago'. In that earlier period, he points out, there was a strengthening in the organisation of workers and increasing resort to strikes or threats of them which were often successful in achieving their objectives. However, the growing power of organised labour received some very severe checks after 1914: in the UK, apart from the war itself, there was the severe post-war slump, the relatively depressed 1920's, the failure of the General Strike in 1926, and the Great Depression of the 1930's. Consequently 'that the process continued (after 1948) for two decades without a pay explosion must also be attributed to the persistence of attitudes that had been inculcated by the hard times before the war. It was in that world that the outlook of the great majority of the labour force of 1950 had been formed'. (op. cit. p. 19).

This view of the matter not only explains why wage increases were (by later standards) so moderate in the 40's, 50's and throughout most of the 60's, but also why moderation was replaced by a more militant attitude thereafter. To quote Brown again

As the norms that custom had provided were left behind, every entitlement became an open question. Meanwhile experience showed that rises in pay that had been resisted as too big to be viable were in fact compatible with the maintenance of employment and a progressive rise in the standard of living. There seemed no reason why the next rise should not be bigger still. (p. 18).

By 1968 only a quarter of British employees had had any experience of employment as adults in the years when jobs were reckoned as hard tc get as they were before the war. In country after country the time must have come when the number with solely postwar experience attained a critical mass, sufficient to outweigh the force of tradition and the respect accorded to older men. It was not within the younger man's experience that they need be restrained in pressing their claims by fear of losing their jobs. They had a new capacity for self-assertion. We have seen how the independence they felt with regard to the employer they felt also with regard to their union officers, who found themselves increasingly obliged to follow the policies formulated by their members, or were elected because their own militancy was congenial.

It may be that the critical mass of the new outlook had been attained in a number of countries by 1968. In international monetary conditions that were lifting the constraint of the balance of payments from a number of countries at that time, it might have brought a pay explosion in all of them without each owing anything to the example of the others. But it is also likely that the French students' revolt, itself emblematic of the repudiation of traditional authority by a younger generation, together with the big general rise in pay that followed it in France, was the spark that set the explosion off in other countries. (pp. 19–20).

Goldthorpe (1978), looking at inflation from a Sociologist's viewpoint, also stresses the growing militancy of organised workers:

I would maintain that over recent decades the generally rising rate of inflation reflects a situation in which conflict between social groups and strata has become more intense and also to some extent more equally matched, with these two tendencies interacting in a mutually reinforcing way. Less advantaged groups and strata have tended to become more free of various constraints on their actions in pursuit of what they see as their interests; hence, they have become more likely to 'punch their weight'—to press their claims closer to the limits of the power they actually possess; and in turn then, they have become more effective in their conflicts with other parties, gaining in this way not only immediate advantages but also a stronger position from which to fight for further claims.

Both of the views quoted seem to imply that the long post-war period of low unemployment and only moderate inflation carried within itself the seeds of its own destruction. It was just *because* it was so favourable to organised labour that it broke down. Labour was organised so as to press its claims for higher wages to the point at which strong resistance was felt—essentially a trial and error process, since this was the only way to discover the limits of bargaining power. It was this which led, first, to accelerating inflation and, then, by way of government reaction, to higher and higher unemployment as the apparently only effective means of countering wage push. Other methods were, of course, tried by both political parties, but their successive incomes policies broke down just as their predecessors had done. Hence the resort to the last shot in the locker—letting unemployment rise.

CHANGING PRICE EXPECTATIONS

Let us now turn to a monetarist interpretation of the same events. This places less emphasis on the attitudes of trade union members and leaders, and changes in their militancy, and more on changing expectations about future increases in prices and wages. We must first introduce the concept of the *natural level of unemployment* which is central to the monetarist analysis. If unemployment is at its so-called natural level, then the rate of increase of wages and prices will be constant (apart from outside shocks, such as those resulting from the oil crisis). If unemployment is below this level, then the rate of increase of wages and prices will tend to accelerate, while with unemployment above its natural level there will be deceleration. The level of unemployment at which the rate of increase of wages tends neither to accelerate nor decelerate has been called the 'natural level' because of its stability properties and by analogy with Wicksell's 'natural rate of interest'. This is the only sense in which it is 'natural'.

The natural level of unemployment may change for a variety of reasons similar to those we discussed in chapter 2 as affecting frictional unemployment. Before 1914, when there was no long-term trend in prices up or down, unemployment averaged about $4\frac{1}{2}$ per cent (although the comparability of that figure to current rates of unemployment is doubtful). Presumably this must have been its natural level at that time. Between the wars, as we saw in chapter 3, it averaged about $10\frac{1}{2}$ per cent. One might think that this was well above the natural level, but there was no clear tendency for the rate of wage increases to decelerate. The explanation may have been three-fold. First, there were large structural changes in the economy which led to a severe contraction of certain industries (e.g. cotton textiles and shipbuilding) and this may have increased the natural level of unemployment. Secondly, although there was a downward trend in prices, expectations may have been slow to adjust to this. Thirdly, there may have been a strong resistance to nominal wage cuts, even though prices were falling and were expected to fall.

In the years 1948–66 unemployment, at 1.7 per cent on average, was almost certainly below the natural level. Yet throughout this period there was no clear tendency for prices or wages to accelerate. The explanation may again have been a very slow adjustment of expectations. As a result of the long history of price stability up to 1939, both workers and employers probably expected prices to be broadly stable after the second World War. Stronger demand and lower unemployment would have made workers press for, and employers ready to concede, larger wage increases than before the war, but both sides may have been fooled into believing that these increases were going to be bigger in real terms than they turned out to be.

From 1948 to 1966 weekly *real* earnings of manual workers rose on average at 2.5 per cent per annum. From 1923 to 1938 they rose at only 1.4 per cent per annum.[1] There were also increases in holidays with pay in the post-war years. Hence the much lower level of unemployment was accompanied (as a monetarist would predict) by a faster rate of growth of wages. Furthermore, the rate of *real* increase which wage negotiators *expected* to get was probably much more than 2.5 per cent per annum (a monetarist would argue). The rate of growth of average weekly *nominal* earnings from 1948 to 1966 averaged 6.2 per cent per annum, and, so long as prices were expected to be stable, this was also the rate of increase in *real* earnings which negotiators expected to achieve. Put this way, the lower level of unemployment was consistent with only moderate inflation because wage negotiators thought they were getting real wage increases which were over 4 times as big as they used to get before the war. The contrast is greater still if the comparison is confined to increases in nominal earnings (assuming that negotiators expected price stability both pre-war and post-war). From 1923 to 1938 the trend rate of increase in nominal earnings was zero.

It is difficult to say for how long expectations of price stability persisted. One might think that the London Stock Exchange would reflect the views of a rather sensitive and sophisticated group of persons who could adjust more rapidly than most to the reality of post-war inflation. Yet it was not until 1959 that the dividend yield on ordinary stocks fell below the yield on Consols. In the post-war years until then, the dividend yield exceeded the yield on Consols by about the same amount as it had done in the inter-war period, suggesting that the expected rate of growth of dividends did not include any appreciable allowance for inflation. In 1959 investors apparently realised that inflation was here to stay, and bid up share prices accordingly, and ever since then the dividend yield has been below the yield on Consols.[2] If, then, investors were not, apparently, allowing for inflation until 1959, wage negotiators may not have been either, and perhaps not until much later. The fact that they were able to secure much higher nominal increases in pay in the post-war years may then have deceived them into thinking that these were going to be much higher real increases. This is, presumably, how a monetarist might explain the failure of inflation to take off from 1948 to 1966, despite the persistently low level of unemployment.

Inspection of Col (1) of Table 2.1 shows that the increase in nominal wages (used here as a short-hand for all incomes from employment per employee in employment) did not start to accelerate markedly until 1969–70, when it shot up to 12.9 per cent, giving a rate of increase in real wages well above past experience of 5.9 per cent, and all this despite a continued upward drift in unemployment. It is noteworthy that Brittan and Lilley (1977) regard this episode as 'The only serious possible example of collective union wage pressure in defiance of apparent market forces' (p. 159).

All this can, however, be reconciled with a monetarist standpoint if one believes that the wage push was due to a growing realisation that inflation was here to stay. For a given degree of tightness of the labour market, then, bigger wage increases were demanded and secured because both sides to the negotiations recognised that prices and other wages were going to go on increasing in the future. Hence it was (on this view) changing price (and wage) expectations which caused the acceleration in wage increases. If this *is* the explanation, however, one cannot attribute the acceleration in wage inflation in the UK in 1967–70 in any simple way to lax monetary policy *at that time*. Rather, one has to blame it on lax monetary policy throughout the years 1948–66, Nemesis having held her hand for so long thanks to the slow perceptions and sluggish response of the British people.

Wages continued to grow at about 12 per cent per annum until 1973–4, when they exploded again, this time to 21 and then, in 1974–5, 31 per cent per annum. Up to 1972 unemployment continued to rise, reaching a post-war high of 3.8 per cent in that year. Since wages showed no signs of *decelerating*, a monetarist might be inclined to take the view that 3.8 was still below the so-called natural level of unemployment, i.e. the level consistent with a constant rate of wage increase. This would also help to explain why the rate of increase accelerated further in 1973–4 and 1974–5, since unemployment fell then to 2.7 per cent—presumably even further below the natural level. It must also be remembered, as we saw in chapter 2, that vacancies in both 1973 and 1974 were unusually high, despite the historically high unemployment. Some of the acceleration in wages must also have been due to accelerating price expectations. Nevertheless, the rate of *real* wage increase in these years was well above the norm of post-war years, and so one must fasten a good deal of responsibility still on unemployment being less than the natural level it seems. The deceleration of wage increases in 1975–6 and 1976–7, accompanied by real wage *reductions*, was, again on a monetarist view, primarily due to rising and high unemployment, now presumably in excess of the natural rate. However, that would put the natural level at around 4 per cent, and it would be difficult to justify a figure as low as that at the time of writing. Unemployment now stands at over 6 per cent, and wage increases have accelerated once more. They averaged about 9 per cent in the year ending mid-1977 but are expected to average well above this in the following year. This acceleration can hardly be attributed to expectations that non-wage elements in prices are going to accelerate—the reverse is more likely. It might be attributed to the usual post-incomes policy reaction, but in that case the fall in the rate of growth of wages in 1975–6 and 1976–7 must also have owed something to incomes policy. Hence one could still make out a case for a natural level of unemployment as high as 6 per cent.

THE GROWING TAX BURDEN

We have, in the above analysis, thus far omitted one factor whose importance has been emphasized by a number of people and notably by Bacon and Eltis (1978). The rates of change of real income from employment in Table 2.1 are all shown *before* deduction of income tax and social security contributions. The relevant changes from the point of view of the recipient are in real wages net of these imposts, but, unfortunately, estimates are not readily available. Bacon and Eltis (1978, pp. 212–3) gave a calculation for a hypothetical worker, married and with no children, earning the same as the average adult male worker in full time employment covered in the Department of Employment April enquiries. His real earnings, before and after deducting the imposts, changed in the way shown in Table 4.1. It is clear that in most years real earnings after deductions increased more slowly than real earnings before deductions. This growing tax burden tended to increase the pressure for wage increases at any given level of demand for labour, according to Bacon and Eltis.

TABLE 4.1

Percentage Changes in Real Average Earnings Before and After Deduction
of Income Tax and Social Security Contributions 1963–75

	April to April of years shown				
Year	Before deduction	After deduction	Year	Before deduction	After deduction
1963–64	6.6	4.0	1969–70	4.6	2.4
64–65	1.1	−1.1	70–71	1.2	2.0
65–66	4.0	2.8	71–72	4.9	6.3
66–67	−0.8	−1.4	72–73	5.8	3.8
67–68	2.8	1.3	73–74	−1.1	−3.9
68–69	3.2	1.8	74–75	4.3	−0.1

SOURCE: Bacon and Eltis, 1978, pp. 212–3. See text for explanation. The
big discrepancy between the fall of 1.1 per cent in real earnings
before deductions from 1973 to 1974 and the increase of 5.9 per
cent in real income from employment per worker shown in
Table 2.1 is presumably due to the fact that the fall refers to
April 1973 to April 1974, whereas the Table 2.1 figures refer to
annual averages. The wage explosion in 1974 came mostly after
April (see the chart in Brittan and Lilley, p. 168).

THEORIES OF WAGE DETERMINATION

The above analysis probably does less than justice to the approaches
described. It is admittedly painting pictures with a broad brush.
Let us, nevertheless, stand back and see what are the main features
of each. We need some sort of theory about what determines the
rate of money wage increases, and into which we can fit the preceding
explanations.

No-one would pretend that wages in the UK are determined by
supply and demand for labour working in a competitive and atomistic
market for individual jobs. Collective bargaining is too obvious and
important to ignore. An economist's approach to an analysis of
this situation would be to ask how the various parties to a wage
negotiation ought to behave if they wished to promote the interests
of the people they represent. The difficulty is, as usual, that if one
wants to be realistic one soon appreciates that there are a great
many important factors to be taken into account. The list which
follows is not exhaustive, and expresses each factor, assumed to

be influencing a particular wage settlement, as if it were acting in the direction of increasing the size of that settlement:

1. Larger wage increases expected elsewhere.
2. Larger price increases expected elsewhere.
3. Increased difficulty of hiring workers at existing wages.
4. Reduced difficulty of finding alternative employment at existing wages.
5. Higher real wage (after tax) which, taking account of price increases expected, workers are determined to get.
6. Workers' increasing 'militancy': e.g. belief that a larger *share* of value-added should accrue to them, and lessened fear that the results of pushing for this will be adverse.
7. Greater readiness on the part of employers to absorb wage increases, because their own profit margins are high, or to pass them on as price increases, because other firms' profit margins are high, or because the firm is in a less than fully exploited and stronger monopoly situation (increased cost to employers of resisting a strike works in a similar way).
8. Lower cost to workers of being on strike, e.g. because of availability of more generous state benefits, more strike pay, more private savings of worker, or better access to credit.
9. Attitude of other bodies (government, the press, BBC, other trade unions etc.) either favours a higher wage settlement, or at least opposes it less strongly.

Let us now attempt to classify the different explanations of the UK's post-war experience in terms of the above factors. Most theories probably admit that most factors could be of *some* importance. What we want to state, however, are those factors which each theory stresses as being of *most* importance.

Before doing this, however, we must deal with the first two factors on our list. We put them first because at any given time they will be the most important determinants of wage increases. In any wage bargain, the most important thing to know is the outcome of other wage bargains, especially those which refer to groups of workers whose pay is commonly compared with those of the workers under consideration. Relativities can change, but there is much resistance to change, and workers and their leaders will feel that they have suffered a defeat if they have secured smaller increases than those negotiated by others with whom they are in the habit of comparing themselves. This means that in any given period (or wage-round, if such a thing really exists) it is very important to know 'the going rate', since most wage increases will cluster quite closely round it.

While all this is very true and for some purposes (e.g. prediction of the outcome of particular wage bargains) very important, it does *not* provide us with an explanation of why wage increases are sometimes greater and sometimes smaller. For this we have to know what it is that determines the 'going rate', and the answer to that may be found in factors which seem relatively unimportant in any *particular* wage bargain, where what chiefly matters is the going rate itself. An analogy may help to make this clear. Imagine an enormous and massive flywheel which is driven by a small engine, and which is also attached to a rather weak brake. At any given time, if we want to predict the angular velocity of the flywheel a short period ahead, the most important thing to know is its present angular velocity, since they are unlikely to differ very much. If, however, we want to understand how the flywheel has reached its present velocity from a period some considerable time ago when it was at rest, we must consider how the small engine has accelerated it. Likewise, if we want to know how we can once again bring the flywheel to rest, we must examine the brake. Neither accelerator nor brake will have much effect on the flywheel in the short-run, but in the long-run they are what really matter.

This analogy is far from perfect. The rate of wage increases, as Table 2.1 shows, can be changed quite rapidly from one year to the next. Nevertheless, it may serve to illustrate our point, and to justify our neglect of the first two factors in what follows. These factors are really common to all sensible theories of wage determination. What distinguishes the theories from each other is what they regard as controlling the accelerator and the brake.

(a) *Monetarist theories*

These stress supply and demand in the labour market, factors 3 and 4 above. It is argued that there is some market situation where the ease or difficulty of finding workers or jobs is such that wage increases will be steady, neither accelerating nor decelerating. In this situation, there will be some unemployment and some vacancies, because of 'frictions'. This level of unemployment has been christened the 'natural level', as has already been explained. The natural level of unemployment can change, but monetarists do not emphasize the other factors listed above as determining it. Rather, they mention such things as restrictions on entry into particular occupations or industries, the efficiency of employment exchanges, housing policy, the speed of structural change in the economy and so on. How high is the natural level of unemployment in Britain? According to Laidler, writing in about 1975, 'preliminary results of work in progress at Manchester University suggest that it is perhaps a little less than 2 per cent in Britain, although such an estimate is necessarily subject to a wide margin of error' (Friedman and Laidler, 1975, p. 45). Writing a little later, Flemming (1976, p. 57) put the natural level in the period 1952–65 between 1¾ and 2 per cent, but remarked 'it has probably risen since 1966 for the reasons mentioned'. These reasons were, first, the increase in the ratio of unemployment benefits to average earnings, and, second, the (growth) of 'an identifiable subculture dedicated to making the most of the welfare system'. No estimates are, however, given. As mentioned in chapter 2, Laslett's estimates suggest that these factors might have increased unemployment by around 1 per cent, which could make the natural rate about 3 per cent. However, our admittedly superficial analysis of the events of recent years suggested it would be at least 4 per cent and could be even 6 per cent. Flemming's (and possibly also Laidler's) estimate for 1952–65 is probably on the low side since it does not allow for the possibility that that was a period of disequilibrium in which negotiators persistently underestimated future inflation. But unless one does allow for that, it is not easy to explain in monetarist terms the acceleration in wage increases since then. One has to assume very big increases in unemployment due to the 'reasons mentioned'.

The implication of the monetarist theory is that the attempt to increase demand so as to reduce unemployment below the natural level will only lead to accelerating inflation, and make it necessary to hold unemployment *above* the natural level for some time to restore inflation to an acceptable rate. The only constructive policy is to lower the natural level by improving the working of the labour market so that 'frictions' are reduced.

The main criticism which can be levied against some leading monetarists (notably Friedman) is that their underlying model of the determination of wages is just (or mainly) one of supply and demand. It does not give sufficient recognition to the existence of collective bargaining. Friedman is reluctant to credit strong trade unions with the power to create *continuing* inflation. In fact, he has said that they cannot do so. He is nevertheless prepared to admit that they can increase the natural level of unemployment, and that they can force up wages and so place the government in the dilemma of choosing between allowing inflation to incur or unemployment to increase. In this way they can influence monetary policy in an inflationary direction, and there is no doubt that Friedman believes that monetary policy can cause continuing inflation (see Friedman and Laidler, 1975, pp. 30–33). It seems to the writer that it is then a matter of semantics, which could be misleading, to say that strong trade unions have not the power to create continuing inflation. Democratic governments are subject to many influences, as they should be if they are to be democratic. If one powerful influence to which they are subject pushes them in the direction of an inflationary monetary policy, it is surely only plain English to say that that influence has caused the inflation?

(b) *Target income theories ('marksman')*

These, as their name implies, stress factor 5 above. Workers' collective bargaining strength is such that they can pretty well secure any wage increase they like. They settle for an increase which will yield a target level of real income (which increases through time), provided their price expectations are fulfilled. If this target level is too high in relation to productivity, the result will be inflation, a disappointment of price expectations, and pressure for an even bigger nominal increase next time—and hence accelerating inflation. The implication is that the way to slow down inflation is to make sure that wage earners get real increases in wages which are rather bigger than they were aiming at. Hence measures to raise productivity, or reduce the tax burden by cutting government expenditure (assuming that workers do not regard £1 of 'social wage' as good as £1 of private wage), or using the proceeds of North Sea Oil for this purpose, are all indicated. Some have even maintained that the expansion of aggregate demand will achieve the desired result, since it will increase output and so enable real consumption expenditures of workers to increase, and this will damp down wage demands.

It is difficult to reconcile these theories with events in recent years. Real wages have fallen at a time when the rate of increase in money wages was also falling. What made workers accept such modest targets? There is also some difficulty in explaining why the faster growth in real wages post-war than pre-war was accompanied by faster money wage increases, rather than slower ones. All this suggests that targets may be moveable, and points to the need for a theory of how they are fixed. Such a theory must surely allow some of the other factors we have mentioned an important part.

(c) *Militancy theories ('militants')*

Some of these stress factor 6 above, which is *not* the same as 5, although it might appear to be so at first blush. The difference becomes clear when one considers the effect of faster increasing productivity on inflation. With target theories, this must directly reduce inflation (unless the target levels themselves are adjusted in the same proportion as changes in productivity, which is not what target theorists assume, so far as the writer knows), whereas with militancy theories the effect, if any, is indirect (see chapter 7.) In addition, militancy theories stress the importance of factors changing employers' resistance to strikes,(7 above) and the costs of striking for workers (8 above). Factor 9, the attitudes of other bodies, also becomes more important since it may influence the resistance of either side in a wage negotiation, and may also influence the outcome of a strike. One has to remember that neither side is monolithic, and the arguments between doves and hawks may be swayed by factor 9. Furthermore, in many important negotiations private employers are not involved, but rather the government either directly or through its agencies. Government's attitude then becomes obviously important, and democratic governments are influenced by the Press and public opinion.

Just as with target theories one can ask what fixes the targets, with militancy theories one wants to know what determines militancy. Some are sceptical of the concept at all. Thus Flemming (1978) says 'The reason that economists are so unsympathetic to appeals to trade union 'militancy' is that it suggests that the intensity of feelings and the urgency of demands matter. This is not possible in the economists' world where everyone maximises. Trying harder makes no difference; only changes in relative intensities of preference matter. In this context increased militancy only leads to higher wages if it reflects either a shift in preferences away from employment and towards the incomes of those employed, or a diminished distaste for confrontation and strike action'. One might reply (a) that there has been a reduction in the penalties attaching to strike action; (b) that there may have been a shift in tastes; and (c) that even without such a shift there could have been more militancy because younger workers gradually learned that its consequences were not as bad as their elders had warned them it would be—in short, as a result of the *trial and error* process described above. This could be described as cautious maximisation in the face of uncertainty.

Nevertheless, once one admits that there *is* a trial and error process, one is close to admitting that supply and demand in the labour market, factors 3 and 4, have some influence. Employers' resistance will be weaker if it is difficult to hire labour, and workers may be more confident in holding out for a bigger wage increase if unemployment is low. Yet some militancy theorists are reluctant to admit that anything resembling the Phillips curve exists. This famous curve purports to show a relation between the rate of wage increases and the level of unemployment, with wages increasing faster the lower is unemployment. Suitably augmented by allowing for changing expectations about the 'going rate' of wage or price increases (i.e. allowing for factors 1 and 2) this curve is central to the monetarist concept of the natural level of unemployment, a concept which is anathema to some militants. If one asks why the rate of wage increases decelerated in 1975–6, one is firmly told that it was nothing to do with the rapid increase in unemployment.

The alternative explanation provided is that workers and their leaders were afraid of inflation itself, and realised that the wage increases of 1974–5 were accelerating inflation, and so must be brought down. On this view, then, the brake is provided by inflation itself, not by unemployment (nor by falling profits). The implication for policy would appear to be that demand should be increased so as to lower unemployment and increase profits and investment, since this will not appreciably affect inflation. The latter will settle down at whatever level workers and their leaders find tolerable—although this may change from time to time, and may be subject to *some* outside influence through factors 7, 8 and 9. It may also be influenced by the extent of wage anomalies, themselves often the result of incomes policies. If anomalies have to be corrected, this will require a faster average rate of increase of wages, since the corrections will generally come about through bigger increases for some, rather than smaller increases for others. Our term 'militants' therefore covers quite a wide variety of positions.

(d) *A synthesis of these theories ('mixers')*

Probably most people who have considered the matter carefully would agree that there is some element of truth in all the theories of wage determination we have outlined. Let us then try to synthesise them. In chapter 8 we present a diagrammatic exposition of the synthesis, and use it to explain the course of events in this country since the war as well as to analyse the policies suggested in chapter 7. Here we content ourselves with a verbal presentation.

At any given time negotiators on both sides will have some idea of the 'going rate' of wage increases, and this will largely determine the outcome of the negotiation. However, what we really want to know is: why is the 'going rate' getting bigger—or smaller?

On grounds of inherent plausibility and on the historical record it is surely true that supply and demand factors in the labour market have some influence. However much one may dislike unemployment, that is no reason for denying that it may influence the outcome of wage negotiations.

However, it is certainly not the only important factor. If wages were determined in the same way as the price of tomatoes, the prosperity of employers would be no more relevant than the prosperity of tomato consumers. It would influence demand, but if, at the level of demand thus determined, there was excess supply as shown by a high level of unemployment or tomatoes left to rot in the greenhouses, then wages would fall just as would tomato prices. Some wages are determined a bit like that, and a larger proportion of all wages may be in some countries than in others. In the UK, however, national wage bargains, including some very important ones in the public sector, are not determined like that. The outcome may be *influenced* by the level of unemployment, especially since this does have a big effect on *some* wages and also, especially via the foreign exchange rate, on some prices. But it is also influenced by other things. Amongst these, in the private sector (and even in some nationalised industries), one must include profits. Employers will be readier to make concessions if profits are high than if they are low, both because they can absorb the cost increases more readily themselves and because they can pass them on more easily if their customers (who are often other employers) are making high profits as well. Workers will push harder if they know that this is so. In the past, profits have generally been high when unemployment has been low, so that it is difficult to disentangle their separate influence on wage increases. Nevertheless, they need not always move inversely. Profitability has been high in some countries even when unemployment was high (e.g. post-war Germany and Italy?) and low when unemployment was low (e.g. Sweden in recent years). Hence they should be considered separately. A 'mixer' would believe that either low unemployment or high profits would tend, *cet. par.*, to accelerate the rate of increase of wages.

So far we have mentioned factors 1, 2, 3, 4, 6 and 7. Factors 8 and 9, the cost of being on strike and the attitude of the government, the press etc. will also influence the outcome of national wage bargains, especially in the public sector (and the public sector covers over 7 million workers, about a third of the total and probably over half of all trade unionists). It is doubly difficult to believe that wages in much of the public sector are determined like the price of tomatoes, nor can profits be of great importance for most of it. Naturally, comparability with private sector increases will be important, but that is merely pointing to the importance of the flywheel and not helping us to understand why it speeds up or slows down. We need to explain why public sector workers succeed in getting more or less from their employer, the government, *given* the expected rate of increase of wages in the private sector. Out of the complex of historical factors involved we may select two as being of sufficiently general importance to justify their inclusion in our theory.

First, the rate of inflation itself. The higher this is, the more likely is the government to resist wage increases since it will be able to count on popular support. Furthermore, it is possible that union leaders and their members will themselves be readier to accept smaller increases after experiencing a bout of high inflation. This is an explanation which is commonly offered for the restraint shown by the West German trade unions whose memories stretch back to the hyperinflation of the 1920's and the (largely suppressed) inflation of the war and immediate post-war years. It is also, as we have seen, an explanation which has been offered for the reduction in the rate of wage increases in this country in 1975–77. The main doubt must be whether the rate of inflation required to produce this reaction will itself grow with inflation. Will it be like a drug which requires larger and larger doses to produce the same effect? Or does our recent experience demonstrate that 30 per cent wage increases and 25 per cent price increases are enough, and will always be enough, to do the trick?

The second factor has already been mentioned, namely, the level of unemployment. The higher this is the less difficulty will the government have in resisting wage demands in the public sector for the same reasons, essentially, as would any employer in the private sector.

While these two factors are important enough to include in a general theory, it must be recognised that there will always be particular factors which may be of great importance at particular times. Thus the oil crisis strengthened the bargaining power of the miners in 1973–4, and this started off the chain of events which led to the general election in 1974, the defeat of the Conservative Government, and the election of a Labour Government committed to destroying the former's wage policy, all of which undoubtedly helps to explain the subsequent wage explosion. There will always be exogenous factors like this which cannot be explained within a usable theory, but that only limits, without destroying, the usefulness of the theory.

Let us now try to summarise. The rate of wage increases will be largely determined by current expectations about wage and price increases, which must be, in the main, historically determined. However, what matters for the long run is that wage increases may be accelerating or decelerating, and here the most important factors involved are: supply and demand in the labour market as measured, e.g., by the level of unemployment; the profitability of firms; the cost of being on strike; and the attitude of workers, the media and the government, which in turn will be much influenced by the rate of inflation. Collective bargaining is a cautious trial and error process. Starting from the current 'going rate of increase' there will be a tendency for this to rise (i.e. for the rate of increase of wages to accelerate) until resistance is felt to be strong. Some sort of balance will then be struck between profitability and unemployment, the point of equilibrium being determined by the cost of being on strike and the attitude of workers, the media and the government.

However, we have not yet included in our mixture the essential ingredient provided by 'marksmen'. Thus suppose we were comparing two economies which were the same in regard to all the other factors we have listed, but in one of which productivity was rising faster than the other. Then, according to a marksman, money wages would eventually rise more slowly in the economy with the faster growing productivity. Workers would press less hard, given all the other factors, because their real wages were increasing faster.

CONCLUSION

In this chapter we have tried to understand how it was that low unemployment was combined with a moderate rate of inflation from 1948 to 1966, and why the two no longer became compatible thereafter, so that inflation increased even though unemployment did as well. Various explanations have been considered, including those provided by 'militants', 'monetarists' and 'marksmen', and we have seen how theorists of each of these persuasions would explain the determinants of wage increases more generally. We have also sought to combine these different theories into a mixture which does, we hope, take account of all the important general determinants of wage increases. A diagrammatic analysis is provided in chapter 8 for those who like such things.

Each of the theories has its implications for policy. We consider these in chapter 7, but, before doing so, we must try to fill the remaining gaps in our analysis of past experience. In the next chapter we seek to explain the large increase in structural unemployment since 1966, and in the following one we discuss the role of the balance of payments.

5 Labour-saving versus labour-using investment

In this chapter we seek to account for that part of the increase in unemployment over the last decade which is due neither to factors such as more generous unemployment benefits relative to net of tax earnings ('frictional') nor to deficiency of demand ('cyclical'). We call the remaining part of the increase 'structural'. While this term has been used to cover a wide variety of different factors, all in some way related to the idea of a mismatch between the structure of demand for labour and the available supply, we believe that the important factor in recent years has been an insufficiency of labour-using investment, whose causes in turn we discuss.

OTHER CAUSES OF STRUCTURAL UNEMPLOYMENT

Let us first deal with other possible causes of structural unemployment. We rely on three recent articles: Department of Employment (October 1976), Turvey (Sept.–Oct. 1977), and Gruen (June 1977).

The first of these articles refers to the report of a working party set up by the Department of Employment to study the changed relationship between unemployment and vacancies which is illustrated so vividly in charts 2.1 and 2.2 (taken from that report). Amongst other factors, the working party considered the effect of increases in unemployment benefits (the earnings related supplement, or ERS, which was introduced in October 1966) and redundancy payments following the Redundancy Payments Act which came into force in December 1965. Both effects were thought to be small, and are included in Laslett's figure on which we based our estimate of the increase in frictional unemployment. Two possible demographic explanations for the rise in unemployment can be ruled out as a result of this report. First, it might be thought that the growth in female employment would result in more unemployment because of higher labour turnover rates for women than for men. However, it is clear from Figures 2.1 and 2.2 that what we have to explain is not a growth in female but in male unemployment. Secondly, it might be thought that the post-war baby-boom would have resulted in an increase in unemployment when the babies grew up and came on to the labour market for the first time. However, the shift in the relationship between unemployment and vacancies came about 5 years too late for that explanation. Furthermore, since there were both boy and girl babies, it is not clear why only the former should have become unemployed.

Turvey (Sept.–Oct. 1977) argues that there is no evidence that the industrial structure of employment in the UK has been changing especially rapidly in recent years, and so concludes that there is no reason to suppose that structural unemployment from this cause has increased. His findings for Western Germany, Sweden and the USA are similar, yet total unemployment has increased in all these countries.

Gruen (June 1977) makes a comprehensive survey of several possible causes of increasing structural unemployment in several different countries. He refers to the debate on 'demand structuralism' in the United States in the mid-sixties, in which it was alleged that rapidly changing consumption patterns and/or the evolution of new technologies ('automation') had increased unemployment. A prominent exponent of this view was Killingsworth (1966). There was little agreement about its importance, however, and some well-known economists were strongly critical of it (e.g. Solow, 1964 and 1976). Turvey's study, mentioned above, suggests that it has probably not been very important in the UK. Apart from this, and some other factors we have already referred to, Gruen considers changes in the regional dispersion of unemployment and refers to an OECD study showing that the coefficient of variation of regional unemployment rates tended to decline in the UK from 1960 to 1972, as it did also in Germany, the Netherla.ids and Sweden. There was no discernible trend in Canada, France and Australia, the only country with a rising trend being the USA. He also points out that three wage ratios have tended to rise, namely, those of juveniles to adults, those of unskilled to skilled, and those of women to men. These rises have been due to legislation or incomes policies, or to centralised wage bargaining, and so have not necessarily reflected supply and demand factors. They may, therefore, have led to structural unemployment. However, apart from the effects of minimum wage legislation in the USA, which does seem to have adversely affected the employment of those whose wages were increased, no evidence of the effects of changes in these ratios on employment is cited. In the UK, the rise in the wages of women relative to men certainly does not help to explain why the increase in unemployment from 1966 to 1975 was so heavily concentrated amongst men rather than women. So far as changes in the other two ratios are concerned, it seems doubtful whether they can explain more than a small part of the increase in structural unemployment. Once again, they do not explain why men, rather than women should have been affected. It is true that the unskilled have suffered more than the skilled, but this is to be expected in any falling off in employment since skilled workers can often 'bump down' unskilled workers. Likewise, a contraction in employment prospects is always likely to affect new entrants disproportionately. Employers prefer to run down their labour forces through natural wastage, and so they take on fewer new workers.

None of the factors so far considered really helps to explain Figure 5.1. This, which is reproduced from the Department of Employment report already referred to, shows that up to 1966 both male and female employment in Great Britain tended to rise, with minor fluctuations. After 1966, however, the two series behaved dramatically differently. Male employment plunged downwards, while female employment, albeit with some long periods of stagnation, continued its upward trend. Although both series show the marks of cyclical changes in the demand for labour (eg. the boom in 1973 and subsequent recession), it is quite clear that there must have been some powerful systematic factor which explains their very different trends after 1966. In what follows, we suggest one possible explanation.

CAN MORE INVESTMENT REDUCE EMPLOYMENT?

As we pointed out earlier, Matthew's explanation of how we achieved full employment omitted any discussion of labour-saving versus labour-using investment. His view seems to have been that more

FIG. 5.1   *Employees in employment (Great Britain, quarterly 1959–76)*

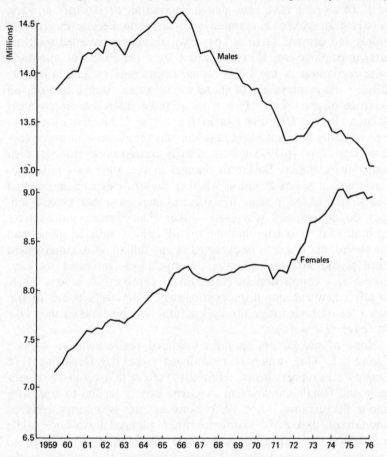

capital must increase the demand for labour. This would indeed
follow from the simple theory of capital and growth which one
finds in some text-books, the idea being that capital is a quantity
rather like labour or land. If you combine a given quantity of
labour with more capital the (marginal) productivity of labour will
be increased. Hence, at a given real wage, more labour can be
employed.

This view of capital does not accord very well with the fact,
familiar to all, that some machines can replace many men. The

simple theory first mentioned must treat this labour saving as being the result, not of more capital, but rather of labour-saving technical progress, which is independent of investment. More realistically, it can be admitted that the technical progress has to be 'embodied' in investment, but its pace—the *amount* of labour required per machine—is still treated as if it was exogenous to the economic system. Hence, at any one time the amount of labour required per machine is given, and is independent of the amount of investment in new machines. The same result follows, then, that the more you invest in any given period, i.e. the faster you add to your stock of machines, the faster will you create new job opportunities. This still does not accord well with experience.

Many commentators have suggested that high real wages in some countries, together with other costs associated with employing workers (notably, social security contributions, which can be very large, fringe benefits, and other costs associated with hiring or firing labour) may have encouraged labour-saving investment, and that this in turn may make it difficult to get back to full employment in some countries.[1] It seems that many people are aware of the fact that more investment can mean *fewer*, instead of *more*, jobs, and that our theory of capital needs to be such as to accommodate this fact. As this is not the place, however, to begin re-writing capital theory,[2] we shall simply proceed in a rather dogmatic way with a theory which, although still representing a great simplification of reality (as must any usable theory) does at least allow for the possibility that more capital can destroy jobs as well as create them. Although we have tried to keep the theoretical exposition to a minimum, some is essential.

A THEORY OF LABOUR-SAVING AND LABOUR-USING INVESTMENT

Let us regard investment expenditure as the cost of changing economic arrangements. This seemingly simple idea has, in fact, extensive and remarkable implications for economic theory into which we cannot enter here,[2] apart from those relating to employment. Let us also assume, for simplicity, that purchased materials per unit of ouput do not change. We can thus confine ourselves to changes in the value of net output and in the cost of labour. Net output, or value-added, consists only of labour costs and profits (gross of depreciation but net of physical maintenance). If change is to be profitable, it must then either increase the value of net output by more than it increases the cost of labour inputs, or else it must reduce the cost of labour inputs by more than it reduces the value of net output. Either of these changes will increase the stream of gross profits. The net return on an investment may then be calculated by relating the increase in profits to the cost of the investment.

The increase in profits resulting from an initial investment will, however vary through time. For a typical enterprise in Britain, one would expect that wage rates would rise faster than the price of output or material inputs. This is only another way of saying that one expects real wages to increase through time. Consequently, if the enterprise were to make no further changes after the original investment, but merely to keep its physical arrangements unchanged, it would see its gross profits gradually dwindle away to nothing. This process is, indeed, the cause of obsolescence and depreciation of capital. Hence the rate of return of the investment is *not* to be found simply by dividing the initial increase in gross profit by the cost of the investment. This would give the right answer only if real wages (and other relative prices) were to remain constant for evermore. Instead, we must allow for the expected increase in real wages (and any other relevant relative price changes) which will limit the economic life of the investment by causing the gross profit from it to dwindle away to zero.

At this point the reader may object that, while this may be true of changes which *increase* net output and labour costs, it is not true of changes which *reduce* net output and labour costs. For the latter, the cost saving will grow and grow and, if it is initially greater than the fall in net output, it will become increasingly so. Such investments should appreciate, not depreciate, because the gross profit from them will grow and grow.

This is a real possibility. However, its practical importance may be limited by two factors. First, widespread imitation of labour-saving improvements, and subsequent further improvements, may cause relative prices of the particular outputs and materials concerned to change in such a way as to reduce gross profits on the original investment to zero. Secondly, the labour-saving improvement will not, in general, go so far as to eliminate employment in the activity altogether. Consequently the rise in real wages will eventually (if no further changes are made) render the activity unprofitable, and so bring the life of the investment to an end as well. False teeth and spectacles are not much use to anyone else once their owner has died.

There are many different possible combinations of output increase (positive or negative) and employment increase (positive or negative) which will yield a profit. Presumably there will be some tendency for the rates of return, at the margin, of all kinds of change to be equalised.[3]

If we are to make any progress we must simplify matters much further. We will therefore assume that only two sorts of change are possible:

Labour-using: Net output increases by a certain amount and so does employment.

Labour-saving: Net output does not change, but employment falls.

We will further assume that both types of investment have the same economic lives, and we will apply our analysis to an activity which bears a fairly close resemblance in some respects to a typical UK manufacturing enterprise. What we want to investigate is the relation between these two types of investment (which must be regarded as representative or averages of many different types), and how in particular they are likely to have been influenced by changes in the share of gross profits in value-added in the post-war period.

At any given time, both types of investment will be undertaken. The change in employment in an activity will then be the net resultant of both, the labour-using investment tending to increase output and jobs and the labour-saving investment tending to reduce jobs. It must be emphasized that *both* kinds of investment are necessary for rapid economic progress. If the attempt was made to confine investment to one kind, without the other, this would slow down economic growth. The first, without the second, would soon find itself running out of labour. Without labour, labour-using investment cannot take place. The second, without the first, would result in stagnant output and falling employment. If we are to have rapid economic progress with jobs growing as fast as the labour force, the right balance has to be found between these two types of investment.

It seems likely that in our economy where investment decisions are decentralized (whether with public or private enterprise), the rates of return on these two types of investment will have to be at least approximately equalised. It is rather easy to show that,

other things being equal, the relative rates of return depend on
the share of gross profits in value-added. The smaller the share
of gross profits, the lower will be the rates of return on both kinds
of investment, but there will be a greater fall in the return on
labour-using than on labour-saving investment at least if we assume
values for the various relevant magnitudes which correspond to those
which would make our model enterprise consistent with a typical
UK manufacturing enterprise. An intuitive explanation of this result
is given in Fig 5.2.

OP represents value-added per annum in some enterprise (or part
of an enterprise). It is assumed for simplicity that this is constant
throughout its economic life, which is OT years. OW represented
the wage-bill in the initial year, so WP is the gross profit in that
year. As time passes, wages rise and so the wage bill absorbs an

FIG. 5.2 *Labour-using and labour-saving investment*

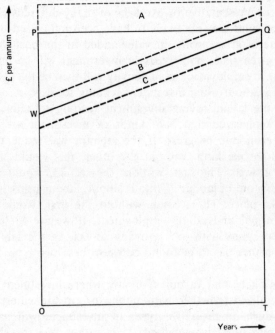

increasing share of value-added. This is shown by the rising line[4] WQ. Eventually, at T, gross profit falls to zero and the enterprises's economic life comes to an end. The triangle PQW then represents the total gross profits received over the whole life of the enterprise.

We now imagine that two investments are undertaken in the initial year which slightly change the enterprise. The first is labour-using, and output increasing. This adds approximately the area A to receipts and also the area B to the wage-bill over the whole life of the project. It thus increases profits over the whole life by A–B (the economic life of the enterprise would be slightly increased, but we neglect this here). The second is labour-saving. This simply saves wages equivalent to C, which is thus its contribution to profits over the whole life of the enterprise. If both investments had the same cost, and if the discount rate were zero, then they would contribute the same amounts to the net present value of the enterprise if

$$A–B = C.$$

Let us keep these simplifying assumptions for the moment, and ask what happens if the initial share of profits is smaller because wage rates are higher, but everything else is the same (that is, if each investment costs the same and increases or reduces output and employment by the same physical amounts; we also assume that value-added is the same). A smaller share of profits initially means that W is higher up. If wages increase through time as before, then the enterprises's life will be shorter, that is, Q will be more to the left. There are then two effects of a rise in wages in the initial position on the additional profits resulting from our two kinds of investment. There is, first, this shortening in life which reduces areas A, B and C all in the same proportion.[5] Given the above equation, this does not affect the *relative* yields of the two kinds of investment. Both will fall by the same amount. Secondly, however, whereas the vertical thickness of A will be unchanged, that of both B and C will be increased, because the same physical change in numbers employed will now cost or save more per annum, since wage-rates are higher. The increase in B tends to lower the yield of labour-using investment, the increase in C tends to raise the yield of labour-saving investment. The net result is, therefore, that although (given the figures we have assumed for illustration below) yields on both types of investment fall, that on labour-using investment falls much more. If the investments were equally attractive before, they are no longer so. One can therefore assume that a fall in the share of profits will tend to reduce both kinds of investment, but especially labour-using investment. It will therefore tend to reduce the rate of growth of both output and employment.

Table 5.1 illustrates the sort of effect one might expect to find

TABLE 5.1

Ratio of Profits to Value-Added and Rates of Return on Labour-Using Versus Labour-Saving Investment: Illustrative Calculation

Profits as a % of value-added	Rate of return, % p.a.	
	Labour-using	*Labour-saving*
35	13.7	11.5
30	10.9	10.9
25	6.8	9.3
20	−0.1	5.6
15	−12.9	−2.8

SOURCE: See Appendix.

on rates of return. We have taken figures which we believe are consistent with the magnitudes to be found in UK manufacturing industry, regarded as a whole or on average. Details are given in the Appendix. We have assumed that when profits are equal to 30 per cent of value-added the rates of return are the same, about 11 per cent p.a., on the two kinds of investment. That being so it appears that, when profits fall to 20 per cent of value added, the return on labour-using investment falls approximately to zero, while that on labour-saving investment is still substantially positive at about 6 per cent p.a. These are rates of return to an average investment of each kind. As profits fall there will be less of each, but a greater reduction in labour-using than in labour-saving investment. Assuming diminishing returns to investment, this could restore equality to returns at the margin, and the rate of growth of employment will fall.

Of course the choice between the two sorts of investment and the amount of investment in total will be influenced by other important factors. These include the expected rate of growth of demand in relevant markets, the cost of finance, rates of taxation, political factors, and labour attitudes.

The expected rate of growth of demand will be a key factor in determining labour-using investment, but its importance here can be exaggerated. Even if total demand is not growing, the individual enterprise which is sufficiently competitive can increase its share of the market, and so it can still pay it to undertake output-increasing and labour-using investment. Nevertheless, as it is much easier to sell more on an expanding market, the expected rate of growth must make a big difference to labour-using investment. It may also have a mild effect on labour-saving investment, but in the opposite direction, by changing expectations about the rate of growth of real wages. Thus faster expected growth will tend to stimulate labour-using investment (by reducing the cost of selling more output) but will tend to dampen down labour-saving investment (by shortening the expected life of any project because of the faster expected growth in real wages).

Cheaper finance, lower tax rates, or other investment incentives, will tend to stimulate both kinds of investment. It is not clear that one kind will receive more stimulus than the other. Labour attitudes may be expected to favour labour-using as opposed to labour-saving investment. In so far as labour's power to enforce its preference on employers is strengthened, this will tend to reduce labour-saving investment, but this may also have the unwanted result of reducing labour-using investment as well. As we have already pointed out, *both* kinds of investment are essential for economic progress. If labour-saving investment is prevented, this must eventually bring all progress to a halt.

THE THEORY APPLIED TO CHANGES IN EMPLOYMENT SINCE THE WAR

Bearing these general points in mind, we now briefly review some of the changes in employment, output, investment, profits and wages since the war.

Table 5.2 gives an analysis of employment by seven major industrial sub-divisions from 1948 to 1976. The most striking feature in it is the decline in manufacturing employment compared with the rise in 'public services' (i.e. national and local government, educational, medical and dental services, and other professional and scientific services), to which Bacon and Eltis (1978) have successfully drawn

TABLE 5.2

Employees in Employment U.K. 1948–76

	(Millions at mid-year)				
Industry	1948	1956	1966	1974	1976
1. Agriculture	1.03	0.81	0.58	0.42	0.39
2. Manufacturing	7.19	8.22	8.58	7.87	7.29
3. 'Public industry'[a]	2.96	2.95	2.62	2.20	2.17
4. Construction	1.32	1.41	1.65	1.33	1.27
5. Distribution	2.12	2.53	2.92	2.76	2.71
6. 'Private Services'[b]	2.30	2.32	2.89	3.24	3.34
7. 'Public Services'[c]	2.78	3.11	4.01	4.97	5.33
8. Total[d]	19.64	21.33	23.25	22.79	22.49

	(trend rates of growth[e], % p.a.)			
	1948–56	1956–66	1966–74	1974–76
9. Agriculture	−3.0	−3.1	−4.1	−2.9
10. Manufacturing	1.6	0.5	−1.1	−3.8
11. 'Public industry'[a]	−0.1	−1.1	−2.3	−0.7
12. Construction	0.8	1.9	−2.8	−2.2
13. Distribution	2.1	1.5	−0.7	−1.0
14. 'Private Services'[b]	0.3	2.5	1.7	1.4
15. 'Public Services'[c]	1.3	2.6	2.6	3.5
16. Total[d]	1.0	1.0	−0.3	−0.7

(a) Mining and quarrying, gas, electricity and water, transport and communication.

(b) Insurance, banking, finance and business services and miscellaneous services. Excludes private domestic servants.

(c) Professional and scientific services (including educational, medical and dental), public administration and defence, but excluding H.M. Forces.

(d) Excludes private domestic servants and H.M. Forces. Totals differ from sums of components because of rounding and, for 1948–58, because of method of estimation used, the totals and components being separately estimated.

(e) Obtained by fitting exponential trends to the data for the years shown.

SOURCES: 1959–76, *Department of Employment Gazette*, October 1975 and later issues. 1948–59, linked on at 1959 using *British Labour Statistics Historical Abstract 1886–1968*, Tables 135 and 138 (to take out private domestic servants).

everyone's attention. Until 1966, employment in manufacturing increased, albeit at a decelerating rate, but thereafter it fell — and the rate of fall has accelerated. By contrast, employment in 'public services' has grown at an accelerating rate. The only other one of the seven sectors where employment has consistently increased has been that comprising insurance, banking, finance, business services and miscellaneous services, which we will call 'private services' for short. Together, these two service sectors now employ over a million more people than does manufacturing. In 1948 they employed over two million less than did manufacturing.

It is worth noting that the changing pattern of employment explains by far the greater part of the other striking change in employment trends to which we have already alluded, namely, the tendency for male employment to fall after 1966 whereas female employment continued to rise (with some checks) at least until 1974 (see figures 5.1 and 5.2). This difference in behaviour of male and female employment is the counterpart of the difference in behaviour of male and female unemployment which we noted earlier (chapter 2). Male employment declined, and female increased, not (to any appreciable extent) because there was a switch from male to female workers *within* industries, but rather because employment fell in those industries which happened to be male-dominated (mostly manufacturing, but also agriculture, mining, construction, and transport) whereas employment rose, or did not fall as much, in industries employing an unusually high proportion of females ('public' and 'private' services especially). Details of the calculations made to justify this statement are in the footnote.[6]

How can we account for these divergent trends? So far as the growth in 'public services' is concerned, the explanation must be largely in terms of social and political factors. These services were increasingly demanded for a variety of reasons, but one motive may have been a desire to offset the fall in employment elsewhere. This phenomenon has been observed in developing, as well as developed countries. It provides a solution to the employment problem which evidently has strong attractions, and we return to it in chapter 7.

Within the (mainly) private enterprise marketed sector, the initial rise followed by a decline after 1966 in employment in manufacturing, and the continuing rise in employment in 'private services' throughout the period, fit quite well into the theory of labour-using and labour-saving investment outlined above. Table 5.3 shows that initially profits

TABLE 5.3
Profits*, Investment* and Output in Manufacturing and 'Private Services'†
1948–76

	(average % for periods shown)			
	1948–56	*1956–66*	*1966–74*	*1974–76*
Profits/value added[a]				
1. Manufacturing	34.1	30.9	25.4	15.9
2. 'Private Services'	38.9	37.4	36.0	38.5
Investment/value added[a]				
3. Manufacturing	14.7	15.6	15.3	14.1
4. 'Private Services'	5.2	8.8	11.7	12.7

	1948	*1956*	*1966*	*1974*	*1976*
Output index (1970 = 100)					
5. Manufacturing	47	65	89	109	103
6. Insurance, banking etc.[b]	41	51	82	126	131
7. Misc. Services[b]	79	75	98	107	108
8. Professional & Scientific[b]	50	65	89	115	124

	(per cent per annum)			
	1948–56	*1956–66*	*1966–74*	*1974–76*
Output trend rates of growth[c]				
9. Manufacturing	3.9	3.5	2.6	−2.6
10. Insurance, banking etc.[b]	2.8	4.9	5.3	2.0
11. Misc. Services[b]	−0.2	3.0	1.6	0.5
12. Professional & Scientific[b]	3.2	3.2	3.1	3.8

* Excluding stock appreciation.

† Insurance, banking, finance and business services and 'other services' including private domestic service, but not distributive trades, or ownership of dwellings.

(a) The published series are not continuously comparable over the whole period. The C.S.O. kindly provided comparable estimates over the period 1960–76, and also continuous series for total investment (excluding stock appreciation) back to 1948. Estimates for income from employment, profits net of stock appreciation, and so value-added, were obtained by linking the published series from the 1959 and 1966 Blue Books of National Income and Expenditure at 1955 and 1960. The resulting estimates for manufacturing are more reliable than those for private services.

(b) It is not possible to isolate 'private services'. The industries shown include them as well as some of 'public services'.

(c) Obtained by fitting exponential trends to the data for the years shown.

SOURCES: National Income and Expenditure 1966–76 and earlier issues and the C.S.O. (see note (a) above).

in manufacturing were high, but that their share of value-added tended to decline, particularly after 1966. This should, according to our theory, have discouraged all kinds of investment, but especially labour-using. In fact, however, investment, taking a run of years together, did not fall in relation to value-added to any appreciable extent (and indeed rose in relation to profits) until the severe recession of the last few years (Table 5.3, line 3). It is possible that the long period of high demand and full employment up to 1966 gradually strengthened business confidence and so encouraged investment, including labour-using investment, despite the tendency for profits' share of value-added to fall. After all, compared with the inter-war years, it was a very good time for business. As the share of profits fell more sharply after 1966, and as inflation speeded up, business confidence weakened. However, there are very long lags in investment planning, and so investment was not cut back at all quickly. Eventually, the increasing uncertainties engendered by rapid inflation and the world-wide recession, together with the drastic fall in manufacturing profits, did result in a big fall in investment. Furthermore, growing uncertainty and poor growth prospects would have especially hit labour-using investment. It looked increasingly risky to extend capacity and take on more labour, but, if one wanted to survive at all, it was still necessary to economise in labour, and so continue with some labour-saving investment.

On this interpretation, the switch towards labour-saving investment would have come perhaps several years after 1966. However, there are possible explanations for the failure of investment to fall which would be consistent with an earlier switch—and the fact that employment started to fall from 1966 makes an earlier switch likely. There was, for example, an increasingly generous tax treatment of investment. That would have stimulated total investment but would not have prevented a switch from labour-using to labour-saving investment, since, as we have argued, their relative attractiveness depends on the pre-tax share of profits in value-added. Alternatively, the failure of investment to fall may have reflected a fall in real rates of return looked for on new investments by businessmen (perhaps reflecting low or negative real returns being received by many savers). This too would not have prevented a switch to labour-saving investment. The continuous fall in employment in manufacturing after 1966, and the slower growth of output and capacity (which we discuss further below), are certainly consistant with a switch in this direction.

The behaviour of profits, investment and employment in 'private services' contrasts strongly with that of manufacturing. Profit's share in value added remained roughly constant throughout the period. The share of investment rose, perhaps for the same reasons as those which prevented manufacturing investment from falling—growing confidence, more generous tax treatment and lower real returns looked for on new investment. Employment also grew quite rapidly.

Hence the initial rise followed by a fall in employment in manufacturing and the continuing rise in employment in 'private services' can be explained in terms of differences in the mix of labour-using and labour-saving investment. This must be regarded as only a tentative explanation, as much more work is needed to confirm the hypothesis. Of course, one might explain the differences in behaviour of output and employment between manufacturing and private services as being due to differences in the investment opportunities available to them. It might just have happened that there was an exogenous decline in labour-using investment opportunities in manufacturing, but not in services. This, however, is not so much an explanation as an assertion. One can always summon a *deus ex machina* as a last resort, but we think it is unnecessary to do so. Nor do we find it persuasive to point to examples of new labour-saving technologies in manufacturing as if they provided an explanation. Labour-saving investment has been with us for centuries, and is in any case to be found in services as well as manufacturing. Our hypothesis has the advantage of relating the phenomena which require explanation (i.e. mainly the fall in employment in manufacturing after 1966) to other contemporary phenomena (i.e. mainly the fall in the share of profits in manufacturing).

It would be interesting to see whether a similar theory can be applied to other industries and other countries. So far as other industries in the UK are concerned, the fall in employment in agriculture was of very long standing. The turn-round in distribution from rising to falling employment may have been due to the combination of the Selective Employment Tax and the ending of resale price maintenance. The fall in 'public industry' employment was of long standing, and may also have been influenced by similar factors to those mentioned above. The changes in construction require explanation, but the fall in recent years may have been due to more subcontracting, and a resulting growth of self-employment.

There is some other evidence in support of the theory. Thus the working party set up by the Department of Employment to which we have already referred concluded that the increase in male unemployment after 1966 was due to the fall in male employment which, in turn, was associated partly with a somewhat lower growth of output and partly with a development towards more economical use of labour (Department of Employment Gazette, Oct. 1976, p. 1098). The authors of the OECD Report '*Towards Full Employment and Price Stability*' (McCracken *et al.*, June 1977), are divided as to whether there is reliable evidence of a shift towards what they describe as greater capital intensity as a result of wage costs rising in relation to output prices (paras. 247, 248). They regard an acceleration in the rate of growth of productivity as evidence of rising capital intensity (para. 233), but they apparently do not think there has been any such acceleration in the UK. Their evidence relates to output per man hour in manufacturing from 1957 to 1975 (chart A3, p. 302). However, our own estimates suggest a pronounced acceleration in the rate of growth of output per employee-year in manufacturing (compare line 10 in Table 5.2 with line 9 in Table 5.3, the implied rates of growth of productivity being 2.3 per cent p.a. (1948–56), 3.0 per cent p.a. (1956–66) and 3.7 per cent p.a. (1966–74)). As *annual* hours worked per employee have probably decreased in manufacturing in the latter part of this period, especially on account of longer annual holidays, these figures probably imply an even faster acceleration in the rate of growth of output per man-hour. Hence one can conclude that this evidence may lend some support to the idea that more investment has become labour-saving.

All the same, it must be pointed out that a switch towards labour-saving investment does not *necessarily* imply a faster growth in labour productivity. The idea that it should do so is based on the concept of capital as a stock of capital goods. If the stock is increased *pari passu* with labour, productivity will not increase (capital widening), but if one increases the stock in substitution for labour (capital deepening), then productivity will increase. Our concept is different. Investment does not only mean more capital goods. It means changing economic arrangements. Labour-using investment means changing them with the result that both output and employment increase, and it is very likely that this will result in an increase in productivity, and possibly in a greater increase in productivity than a labour-saving investment which has the same rate of return. In the example given in Table 5.1, this is indeed the case, as the reader who consults the Appendix will discover.

Consequently, we cannot be sure that, because productivity in manufacturing has been growing faster, there must have been a switch to labour-saving investment. The evidence for such a switch is different, namely, a tendency for both output and employment to grow more slowly. Such a tendency is clear from the figures for manufacturing output and employment in Tables 5.1 and 5.2. The only difficulty in interpreting them from the point of view of our theory is the need to allow for cyclical factors, on which we have more to say below.

ANOTHER WAY OF PUTTING IT: TOO HIGH WAGES

There is an alternative way of describing what has happened in UK manufacturing industry. Instead of pointing to the falling share of profits in value-added, as we have done, and drawing conclusions about the effects this has had on the pattern of investment, one can say that *real* wages have increased too fast, and that this has simply reduced employment. The question is, how does one decide what has been too fast an increase in real wages?

Flemming (February 1976 and New Year 1977) has argued that recent increases in real wages have reduced the demand for labour and so tended to increase unemployment, particularly of unskilled workers whose wages have been especially favoured by incomes policy. He points out that real wages increased by more than the *trend* in labour productivity during 1973-4, if allowance is made for the worsening in our terms of trade. This argument is very similar to ours, since, if real wages rise faster than labour productivity, the share of profits in value-added will generally fall, and we have argued that this will result in a slower growth in demand for labour. However, there are some differences.

To make the two arguments equivalent, one should measure changes in what is known as the *product* wage, that is, one should divide an index of money wages by an index of the price of output (value-added in this case) so as to measure changes in the quantity of output paid to workers. One must also correct for cyclical fluctuations, either by considering trends or by taking averages over a sufficient number of years. If both of these are done, it follows that a rise in the real product wage which is faster than the trend rise in real output per man must reduce the trend share of output accruing to profits.

Flemming's figures differ from those we have used in two respects. First, they apply essentially to the whole economy rather than just to manufacturing or private services. Secondly, they measure the real wage in terms of its purchasing power over consumer goods and services rather than over output. Hence our figures, unlike Flemming's, are not open to the counter-argument made by Matthews and King (Feb. 1977) that, taking the economy as a whole, there is no evidence that the real *product* wage rose faster than the trend of productivity between 1970 and the third quarter of 1976. The evidence for a fall in the share of profits in value-added in *manufacturing* seems quite clear over an even longer period than this.

The fact that there has been concern in a number of countries (e.g. Australia, Western Germany and the Netherlands) that 'too high wages', and an associated profits squeeze, have caused increasing structural unemployment suggests that the phenomenon may be a real one. The Netherlands is indeed a more extreme example than the UK. The slowing down in output and employment growth in manufacturing started rather earlier, and profits have been squeezed even further. Models have been constructed to show how the rise in real wages may have led to increased scrapping of old equipment whose profits have been eliminated leading, in turn, to workers being laid off (see Hartog and Tjan, 1976), but these have been criticised on a variety of grounds. The fact remains that unemployment has increased very markedly, employment in manufacturing has fallen and manufacturing output has expanded more slowly, all of which fits our theory.

CYCLICAL VERSUS STRUCTURAL UNEMPLOYMENT

Of course, one might explain the slower growth in manufacturing output in the Netherlands or the UK in terms of cyclical factors, that is, of a slower growth in demand. For this to be a correct explanation, however, it ought to follow that a revival in demand would result in a revival in output. There ought to be spare capacity, or slack, which could then be taken up. *Per contra*, if the structural hypothesis is correct, a revival in demand should not find the capacity there to meet it. Instead of capacity expanding along its previous trend line, the switch to labour-saving investment would have caused it to expand more slowly. Hence the amount of slack would be much less than a simple comparison of actual output and trend output would suggest.

The 1973 boom in the UK provides evidence in favour of the structural hypothesis. If one fits an exponential trend to the series for manufacturing output from 1948 to 1973 one finds that, as expected, the main boom years lie above this trend. Thus output in both 1960 and 1964 was 3.2 per cent above trend, while in 1955, which was probably the strongest post-war boom year (as we have seen, judging by the very low unemployment in that year, and the high level of vacancies, see Fig. 2.1), output was no less than 4.8 per cent above trend. By contrast, in 1973 output was a mere 0.6 per cent above trend. Yet, to judge by the vacancy statistics (Figs. 2.1 and 2.2), 1973 was as strong a boom as 1955. Furthermore, other statistics confirm the high pressure of demand in 1973. The volume of orders on hand in the engineering industries reached record levels at the end of that year, having risen by a third during it, and the volume of imports of goods and services increased by 13 per cent between 1972 and 1973. All this seems to confirm our hypothesis that it was not just manufacturing output but *capacity* as well which grew slowly after 1966.

TOO RAPID EXPANSION IN DEMAND?

Some observers have sought to explain the relatively poor showing of output in 1973, and the evident pressure on the labour market (as shown by the high level of vacancies) and on prices generally, by reference to the suddenness and speed of the expansion (see, for example, McCracken *et al* June 1977, p. 58, and also Department of Employment Gazette, Oct. 1976, p. 1098). The argument seems to be that capacity was in some sense not especially fully utilised, but that the very rapid expansion in demand was the cause of the trouble. However, one might have expected that an unusually rapid expansion of demand, if there was in reality plenty of spare capacity, would have resulted in an unusually rapid growth of output. Yet to judge from previous booms, the expansion of manufacturing output in 1972–3 was not especially rapid. It grew by 8.4 per cent, which is admittedly more than the 6.2 per cent growth in 1954–5 (but then, as we have seen, to a much higher level above trend, so that there should have been less spare capacity to start with in 1954), but not much different from the 8.1 per cent growth in 1959–60, and rather less than the 9.2 per cent in 1963–64.

TOO LITTLE LABOUR-USING INVESTMENT

If firms undertake investment which saves labour rather than increases output, then capacity will only grow slowly and, if demand is suddenly stepped up, they are in no position to meet it. The real amount of slack in the system is less than the high unemployment figures suggest. The situation is quite different from that of a cyclical fall in demand when firms can expect a recovery fairly soon. They will then not discharge their labour, and will stand ready to meet the recovery. But if they do not expect a recovery, and so discharge their labour and adapt their production facilities accordingly, capacity really has fallen.

It is therefore dangerous to project some past upward trend of capacity onwards through a long period of stagnation in output such as we have been experiencing. It is likely that manufacturing capacity has been growing very slowly, and the underlying situation at the time of writing may be similar to that in 1973 in that true spare capacity is much less than either projections of past trends or the unemployment figures may suggest. Some confirmation of this is provided in a recent NEDO paper.[7] One has only to turn to the daily newspapers to find accounts of plans to reduce capacity and discharge labour in British Leyland, British Steel and other large enterprises, private as well as public. The evidence of labour-saving investment is plain to see. Nor is such investment inherently undesirable, on the contrary, it is essential if we want economic growth to continue. What *is* undesirable is the lack of sufficient labour-using investment to complement it.

THE CEPG'S OBJECTION CONSIDERED

In their recent *Economic Policy Review* (Cambridge Department of Applied Economics, March 1978, p. 26), the Cambridge Economic Policy Group have attempted to refute the proposition that too high real wages, or too low profits, in manufacturing industry have caused part of the increase in unemployment in recent years. Their argument is that they can explain by far the greater part of changes in employment in manufacturing in terms of two variables: time and the (lagged) level of manufacturing output. Time represents the trend for labour productivity to increase. The reason why employment has fallen in manufacturing is then simply that output has not grown fast enough to offset this trend (since 1975, employment has, indeed, fallen less than their equation would predict, but this is attributed to the temporary employment subsidy and other job-saving measures).

These results leave little room for a significant influence on manufacturing productivity and employment of any factors other than those already identified. There is no evidence at all of accelerated 'labour-saving'. Nor, apparently, have the rise in fuel prices, low profits, or 'excessive' real wages had any marked effect unless low productivity in 1976 and 1977 (but not before) is attributed to these factors rather than to job-saving measures.

The weakness in this argument is very clear. The CEPG seem to forget that the cause of the slow growth of output may have been (and, if we are correct, was) at least partly the low profits and 'excessive' real wages for which they find little room. Their equation does nothing at all to refute the view put forward in this chapter that low profits led to labour-saving investment and low growth of capacity and output. All it does is to show that employment fell when output grew more slowly, which is quite consistent with our view. Perhaps they expected that more labour-saving investment would lead to a break in the trend rate of growth of productivity. Like some others (see p. 59), they might have expected the trend to accelerate. However, as we have already pointed out, there is no obvious reason why this should be so, although in fact our own estimates suggest that there was some acceleration.

CAUSES OF INADEQUATE LABOUR-USING INVESTMENT

We saw in Chapter 3 how private savings had increased very markedly in the 1970's, but, disappointingly, the economic system had failed to adjust to this so as to raise the share of private investment. It does not look as if we can blame the disappointing performance of private investment in manufacturing (it was not disappointing in services) on a shortage of savings. But nor can we blame it on an abnormal reluctance of investors to take up favourable investment opportunities. Quite the contrary, our task above was rather to explain why it was that investment in manufacturing had held up so long despite the drastic fall in profits and low rates of return (for the latter, see especially Flemming et al, March and June 1976). Hence the finger of blame points neither at savers nor investors, but at whatever it was that caused the fall in manufacturing profits. It seems that this is also the view of the Prime Minister, Mr. Callaghan, who is reported to have said to the Labour Party Conference in September 1976:

> The willingness of industry to invest in new plant and machinery requires not only that we overcome inflation, but also that industry is left with sufficient funds and sufficient confidence to make new investment. When I say that they must have sufficient funds, I mean that they must be able to earn a surplus, which is a euphemism for saying that they must make a profit (*The Times*, 29 September 1976, p. 1.).

Why did the share of profits in manufacturing value-added fall so much, but not in 'private services'? According to the OECD Report already cited there has been a long-term decline in gross rates of return on capital in a number of countries (the USA, Germany, Italy, Belgium and the Netherlands are mentioned, as well as the UK, para. 237). The Report suggests several reasons for this: firms may have been misled by conventional accounting practices into thinking that their profits were higher than they really were so that they did not raise prices sufficiently to cover the higher costs of capital replacement in an inflationary situation; stronger competition, especially on international markets; and domestic price controls and other restrictive policies, (para. 230). All of these probably help to explain the fall in profit margins in UK manufacturing. Banking and services were less exposed to foreign competition, and financial intermediaries' profits probably generally benefit from inflation and a widening margin between borrowing and lending rates of interest.

There nevertheless remains the intriguing possibility that the success or failure of particular industries over this period was in some way more directly connected with the fact that they employed women (for success!) or men (for failure!). Relative wage movements do not suggest that women became relatively cheaper—rather the reverse. They may, all the same, have become 'better buys', whether because of improvements in education, less need for physical strength in many types of employment, or greater willingness to do as they were told. Womens' relative wages, traditionally much lower than mens', may have got out of line with their relative productivity. All this is, however, very speculative. We can probably explain what happened in terms of greater foreign competition for manufacturing as compared with services, and without appealing to sex differences— appealing though they are!

However, while greater exposure to foreign competition may have been the main *proximate* cause of the fall in manufacturing's profitability, it was not the *fundamental* cause. Had the government thought it desirable or feasible, it could have devalued the exchange rate by more than it did. This would have increased the relative profitability of the traded goods sector in the economy (i.e. especially manufacturing) so long as the ensuing rise in prices and profits did not increase wages by enough to offset the initial effects. It was precisely because the government did not want to aggravate inflation, and could not be confident of preventing this offsetting, that it was reluctant to push the exchange rate further down. Price controls may also have restricted profits in some private industries, and, since they were enforced primarily as an anti-inflationary device (mainly with a view to securing trade union leaders' cooperation in incomes policy), they too can be attributed to the same basic cause.

CONCLUSION

In Chapter 4 we argued that, in so far as the increase in unemployment from 1966 to 1977 was due to deficient demand, the government did not choose to prevent it by increasing demand because it feared the inflationary consequences of doing so. We have now reached the important conclusion that much of the rest of the increase in unemployment (i.e. the part which we have called structural) occurred because the government felt unable to increase profits in manufacturing and other industries, by further devaluation of the pound, for the same basic reason. Hence by far the greater part of the increase in unemployment was due to that reason. Low unemployment and high profitability were incompatible, under existing arrangements, with low and stable rates of inflation. Our next task is to consider, in Chapter 7, what changes in existing arrangements might remove, or lessen, this incompatibility. Before doing so, however, we must first deal with the objection that there is another constraint on our ability to get back to full employment, namely, the balance of payments.

6 The balance of payments constraint

In the 1950s and early 1960s the Treasury behaved like a simple Pavlovian dog responding to two main stimuli: One is 'a run on the reserves' and the other is '500,000 unemployed' (Brittan, 1964, p. 288).

The main line of argument is that the entire nexus of inter-related problems stems from loss of export and home markets to foreign competitors, which has meant insufficient export earnings to finance the level of imports which would be purchased at full employment. Since growth of domestic demand and output had to be low enough, on average, to avoid excessive balance of payments deficits, unemployment has risen from one cycle to the next. (Cambridge Department of Applied Economics, March 1976, pp. 1, 2).

The first of these quotations is a vivid description of the situation during the period of fixed exchange rates and full employment which lasted from 1950 to 1966. During these years it certainly seemed to be the case that macroeconomic policy largely consisted of expanding demand until our foreign exchange reserves came under pressure, and then of restricting demand until unemployment became uncomfortably high, by which time the pressure on the reserves had gone. So, once again, demand could be safely expanded until .... This was the famous stop–go cycle. Viewed in retrospect, one wonders why we grumbled about it so much. Unemployment was kept very low, growth was, by our own historical standards if not by those of contemporary Western countries, high, and fluctuations in output were smaller than in many other countries. Hence, although the balance of payments did seem to limit our power to stimulate demand and reduce unemployment, the limitation does not now appear to have been a very serious one.

Given all the other factors in the situation, the reason for this lay in wage restraint. If money wages had risen much faster than they did, and had we kept to our fixed exchange rate with the dollar, we would have been forced to accept higher and higher unemployment or else tighter and tighter import restrictions (or higher and higher import tariffs). As it was, thanks to wage restraint, we did remarkably well.

The pound was devalued in 1967, and was allowed to float against other currencies from August 1971. It might be thought that this would have enabled us to pursue an independent macro-economic policy and so to achieve whatever level of employment seemed best. Having abandoned the fixed exchange rate, our price level was no longer tied to that of other countries. If the balance of payments worsened, we had only to let the exchange rate depreciate by a sufficient amount to restore it to whatever was regarded as a suitable balance. The second quotation above shows, however, that some economists still believed that the balance of payments constraint was operative, despite several years of floating exchange rates. Moreover, unlike in the earlier period of fixed exchange rates, the constraint was now beginning to bite hard. Unemployment had risen far beyond the point at which the Treasury, in Brittan's colourful metaphor, would have started to salivate. There is little doubt that the second quotation still represents the views of an important body of opinion. What is the explanation for this?

One possible explanation is that those who believe in a balance of payments constraint do not believe that depreciation of the exchange rate will remove a deficit. There are two reasons for this which must be carefully distinguished. First, one might believe that, *even if money wages could be kept constant* following a depreciation of the exchange rate, the balance of payments would still not improve. This used to be called 'elasticity pessimism'. It is certainly not supported by most empirical work, and it is not the explanation for the second quotation above. Secondly, one might believe that money wages could not be held constant, and that they would eventually rise as a result of depreciation by enough to cancel out all its effects. Thus if, for example, the exchange rate depreciated by 10 per cent, wages would eventually rise by 10 per cent, as would the sterling price of imports. With costs up by 10 per cent, prices would also rise by 10 per cent, and the *real* situation (i.e. all relative prices) would be back to where they were before the exchange rate had depreciated. There would then be no improvement in the balance of payments.

This view, or something very close to it, does seem to be held by an important body of opinion, including both monetarists and the authors of the second quotation—who are certainly not monetarists. Monetarists take the view that exchange rate depreciation has only a temporary effect on the balance of payments. The balance improves as private holdings of money are increased in order to restore them to the real levels (i.e. in terms of purchasing power) that they had before prices rose. Once real money balances have been restored by this increase in private savings, the latter revert to previous levels and so does the balance of payments. The authors of the second quotation do not subscribe to this monetarist view of the balance of payments, but nevertheless, in the work cited (p. 1), they stressed the inflationary dangers of devaluation:

> Even if international agreement, and assistance, for a large UK devaluation *could* be secured, there would still be no guarantee that a large fall in sterling would be effective unless stringent and permanent limits on money wage settlements were then enforced in Britain to prevent the higher cost-of-living feeding back into labour costs.

For our present purposes, we do not need to consider for what length of time, or to what extent, devaluation does improve the balance of payments. Much would depend on the accompanying macroeconomic policy. Simulation exercises with econometric models of the UK economy suggest that, although wages and prices eventually may rise so as to wipe out the initial competitive gains (according to the assumptions of the models) the balance of payments may improve for several years (after a short initial worsening) (see Ball, Burns and Laury, 1977, and Odling-Smee and Hartley, 1978).

The main point we wish to make is simply that the fundamental problem is nothing especially to do with the balance of payments. It is to do with wages. If devaluation could secure a permanent reduction in wages in terms of foreign currency it could also secure *either* a permanent improvement in the balance of payments at any given level of employment *or* a higher level of employment at any given balance of payments. This assertion does not contradict the conclusions of the econometric models, nor is it inconsistent with the beliefs of the authors of the second quotation, nor with the beliefs of monetarists. Nevertheless, it may help to put matters in their correct perspective. For the problem we are confronted with is the same one as we considered in previous chapters, namely, how can money wages be restrained sufficiently to permit the economy to be run at full employment and with adequate profits?

There should be nothing very surprising about this conclusion. It would, after all, be rather odd if closing the economy to foreign trade were somehow to make it easier to get to full employment. Foreign trade widens the opportunities for employment. Countries with very little foreign trade (such as India) face severe problems in finding employment for their growing populations, at wages which are very low by most standards. Countries with very high foreign trade ratios (such as Hong Kong, South Korea and Taiwan) have succeeded in getting close to full employment with rapidly rising real wages and despite rapidly growing populations and few natural resources. Without foreign trade there is no doubt that their employment problems would have been much worse. Of course, foreign trade may turn sour, and industries which have flourished as exporters for a time may suffer very badly if foreign demand falls away for one reason or another. But that can hardly explain more than a small part of our current employment problem. There seems little doubt that that problem would on balance be much worse if we did not engage heavily in foreign trade. That being so, it only confuses the issue to treat the balance of payments as a major constraint on our ability to achieve full employment. It is not the balance of payments which is the constraint, but our inability to prevent wages from rising too fast when unemployment is low and profits are high.

7 Policies to restore full employment

We can summarize the preceding analysis by listing three conditions which must be fulfilled if we are to restore full employment for any sustained length of time:

1. Aggregate demand must be kept sufficiently high.
2. Wages must not rise much faster than labour productivity.
3. The share of profits must be such that the right mix of labour-using and labour-saving investment is undertaken, given the rate of growth of the labour force.

The fundamental obstacle to achieving these conditions is, and has been, the tendency of wages to rise faster than productivity, and at an accelerating pace, when unemployment is low and profits are high. We consider policies to alter this state of affairs in (roughly) ascending order of their radicalism (we do not, however, consider *very* radical policies).

We have also tried to relate policies to the underlying theories of wage determination which seem to have motivated them, using the classification provided earlier. However, we interpret the terms 'marksman' and 'militant' a little differently. In our earlier discussion we wanted to isolate those aspects of wage determination which different theories emphasize. Consequently, we considered only a 'pure' marksman, or a 'pure' militant, who regarded unemployment as having no bearing on wage determination. It is not always very helpful to stick to these 'pure' concepts in the following discussion. A pure marksman, for example, might dismiss most of what follows as being irrelevant so far as employment is concerned, since much of it is related to the problem of reconciling low unemployment with reasonably stable prices and, for a pure marksman, there is no such problem. Consequently, we use the terms, unqualified, to mean theorists who *emphasize* the same factors as their 'pure' brethren, but who nevertheless admit that unemployment is also of some relevance, if only because governments believe that it is, so that unemployment is reduced when inflation falls. When we want to discuss the implications of a 'pure' theory, we describe it as such.

(a) *Measures to increase aggregate demand*

Not so long ago, the conventional answer to the question 'How can we restore full employment?' would have been 'By increasing demand by fiscal and monetary policy, with the balance of payments being taken care of by exchange rate changes, as required.' The last occasion when this was tried was in 1972–3, when output shot up, and the unemployment rate was reduced from 3.8 to 2.7 per cent. This was followed, however, by accelerating inflation and the worst recession since the 1930s. Whilst one cannot attribute all of that to the earlier expansionary policies, they undoubtedly played some part. This experience must have helped to convince many (including, to judge by the quotation at the beginning of this book, the Prime Minister, Mr. Callaghan) that such policies could no longer be relied upon to secure full employment in the long run.

Monetarists had been saying this for a long time. Indeed, some have recently gone further, and have asserted that expectations are now adjusted so quickly that monetary expansion can no longer count on achieving even a temporary increase in output and employment—its whole effect is simply on prices (see, for example, Minford, December 1977). But one does not have to go so far as that. If expansionary policies bring the level of unemployment down and profitability up to the point at which inflation starts to accelerate, then, sooner or later, the process will have to be reversed. This means that unemployment will have to be raised above the 'natural level' and profitability will have to be depressed, and expectations will have to adjust themselves back to where they were. The net result may be that the expansionary policies have, on average over a run of years, actually increased rather than reduced unemployment.

The monetarist view is, then, that the government cannot, in the long-run and through macroeconomic policy alone, choose the level of unemployment. That level must be the natural level (which can be influenced by other policies), and the government should recognise this. It can then at least use its macroeconomic policy so as to obtain the desired rate of inflation. In current circumstances, that means holding unemployment sufficiently high to make inflation decelerate to the required rate, and then keeping it at the natural level.

Pure militants who believe that the rate of wage increases does not depend to any significant extent on the level of unemployment, but who also admit that profitability does affect wage increases, have to confront the following dilemma. By pursuing a sufficiently expansionary policy which raised the share of profits and reduced that of wages, the government could stimulate labour-using investment. In this way it could gradually eliminate structural unemployment, and also reduce average cyclical unemployment to a desirable level. However, all this would be at the expense of accelerating inflation, since the share of profits required for this purpose would almost certainly be too high to secure wage restraint. Alternatively, by pursuing a sufficiently deflationary policy which reduced the share of profits and raised that of wages, the government could bring down inflation to whatever was thought to be a desirable level. But this would probably require bankruptcies and increasing structural and cyclical unemployment. On this view, then, the government, through its macroeconomic policy, can either have tolerable unemployment at the expense of accelerating inflation, or tolerable inflation at the expense of growing unemployment. To find a *via media* requires resort to some of the other policies considered later on. Macroeconomic policy alone is not enough.

There is one possible escape from this dilemma, although it would require a militant with James Bond's combination of luck and skill to control macroeconomic policy in such a way as to find it. By steadily expanding demand, starting in a situation of depressed activity, it might be possible to generate expectations of faster growth. This in turn might stimulate labour-using investment sufficiently to reduce structural unemployment, despite a low share of profits. The latter would prevent wages and prices accelerating. In this way, unemployment could be reduced to tolerable levels without inflation accelerating. Unfortunately, one must doubt whether this happy combination of circumstances could be achieved through macroeconomic policy alone.

Pure militants who believe that neither unemployment nor the share of profits are important determinants of the rate of wage increases, but that faster inflation will itself eventually lead to some sort of wage restraint, are consistent in advocating expansionary policies. According to their view of the matter, the rate of inflation is largely determined by workers' preferences, the institutional arrangements for wage-fixing, the extent to which wage anomalies need to be corrected (the greater this is, the faster must wages increase), and similar factors. We may as well get the lowest level of unemployment we can, since it will not speed up inflation to do so.

Pure marksmen who believe that the only really important factor is the *real* rate of wage increases are also consistent in advocating expansion. Their argument is that this will provide more resources which can be devoted to satisfying workers' real wage demands. The result will be to reduce the pressure for increases in money wages and slow down inflation.

A mixer who gave a fair amount of weight to both unemployment and profitability as factors influencing the rate of wage increases would reach the same conclusion as the monetarist above. Expansionary measures can be safely pursued, and are highly desirable, up to a certain point. Recent experience suggests, however, that that point is far below the level of full employment as defined in Chapter 2. That being so, expansionary measures by themselves cannot get us back to full employment. Correct macroeconomic policy is a necessary, but not a sufficient, condition to achieve that.

(b) *Import restrictions*

The Cambridge Economic Policy Group (CEPG) (see Cambridge Department of Applied Economics, February 1975, March 1976, March 1977 and March 1978) have for some years now argued that restrictions on manufactured imports, combined with suitable macroeconomic policies to expand demand, and a variety of measures to stimulate investment (especially in manufacturing), are necessary if we are to reduce unemployment to acceptable levels in the long run. They attach great importance to the balance

of payments, and regard it as the main constraint on the growth
of output of the economy over the coming years (as over past
years). The quotation given in Chapter 6 illustrates their view.
The role of import restrictions is then to prevent the balance
from deteriorating when demand is expanded. This will enable
output to grow sufficiently fast to reduce unemployment. It is
noteworthy that the TUC has also advocated expansion of demand
and import restrictions.

There are many aspects of these recommendations which one
might discuss, but we will confine ourselves to two (for a further
discussion, see Corden, Little and Scott, 1975). First, we will
consider why the CEPG prefer import restrictions to the more
orthodox policy of devaluation to deal with balance of payments
problems. It is this preference which constitutes the main difference
between the policies they advocate and straight-forward macroeconomic policies considered in (a) above. Secondly, we will consider
whether the CEPG have really understood the nature of our unemployment problem.

The CEPG prefer import restrictions to devaluation mainly
because they believe that the former would be less inflationary.
It seems that their view of wage-determination is mainly that
of a marksman, although they may also believe, with some militants,
that the share of profits is an important factor:

> In the longer term fast growth of GDP and productivity, achieved
> by means of import restrictions, would reduce prices relative
> to money wages, making a lower rate of inflation easier to
> achieve; after 1980 money settlements of 5% imply improvements
> in the real value of negotiated basic rates. But the strategy
> of progressive devaluation would make low money wage settle-
> ments much more difficult to achieve in the early 1980s, because
> rising import costs would push up prices and erode the real
> value of negotiated basic rates. Moreover, the share of profits
> would be rising fast, especially in export industries. It seems
> most unlikely that wage settlements could in fact be held down
> to 5% in such circumstances. (op. cit. March 1978, p. 19).

It is really the increasing share of profits which constitutes
the important difference between the import restrictions strategy
and that of devaluation. The rising price of imports, which is
mentioned in the quotation, would be common to both. True,

with import restrictions on manufactures only it would be manufactured imports which would rise in price, rather than imports of food, materials or fuels, but that does not make any essential difference. In order to secure the same improvement in the balance of payments, prices of imported manufactures would have to rise much more, and so the effect on the cost of living would probably be much the same. If it were thought that wages were especially sensitive to, say, food prices, it would always be possible, with the devaluation strategy, to subsidise food and tax manufactures so as to produce the same effect (or this could be achieved by failing to devalue the Green Pound, as in the past). However, if it were indeed the case that import restrictions increased the share of profits less than devaluation, then to that extent they would permit faster real wage increases, and would indeed be less inflationary on either a marksman or a militant view of wage determination.

However, before we accept that conclusion we must ask whether profit's share really would increase less? Would not profits in import-competing industries rise following import restrictions? This seems very likely. Furthermore, since import restrictions would almost certainly increase costs and reduce efficiency, there would be a loss of real income here which would have to be borne by someone—either profit receivers or wage-earners. Hence the scope for real wage increases with import restrictions might be no greater than with devaluation.

Indeed, one might ask why, if profits did not increase, would investment and employment increase? It is precisely because it would increase profits in manufacturing that a real devaluation (i.e. one which succeeded in reducing British wage costs in terms of foreign currency) would increase employment. How can import restrictions somehow do the trick with no increase in profits? The CEPG view seems to be that higher profits are not essential to encourage more labour-using investment. We saw this in Chapter 5. However, we also saw that the arguments on which their view is based are without foundation. Hence we conclude that import restrictions would not gain us any more employment than would devaluation, for a given rate of inflation.

The likelihood is, in fact, that import restrictions would do much less for employment. This is partly because of the inefficiencies and higher costs to which they would lead, as already mentioned, and partly because of retaliation by our trading partners. The latter might very well prevent there being any gain in employment at all, since our exports of manufactures could fall as fast as our imports. The CEPG admit that this constitutes a serious argument against their proposal, but presumably they must believe that we have a reasonable chance of avoiding it through negotiations with our trading partners (otherwise it would not make sense to continue advocating import restrictions year after year). If the import restrictions were a temporary response to a crisis, this might well be the case. However, it is an essential feature of the CEPG proposal that the restrictions should be imposed for a long enough period to create confidence in the protected industries and so stimulate investment there. The CEPG have themselves mentioned a period of 10 years or more (op. cit. March 1976, p. 41). It is rather difficult to see how we could continue to be members of the EEC in these circumstances.

So much for import restrictions *versus* devaluation. It does not look as if they possess any magical properties which will somehow solve the problem which, we concluded in (a) above, macroeconomic policy (including exchange rate policy) is alone unable to solve. Let us briefly conclude by asking whether the CEPG have really understood the nature of that problem.

The CEPG regard the balance of payments as the chief constraint on our economic growth and ability to increase employment. We have already argued in Chapter 6 that this is misleading. It seems to suggest that foreign trade somehow makes it more difficult to achieve full employment, whereas the reverse is almost certainly true. Their recipe of import restrictions, which would reduce the importance of foreign trade in the British economy, would not make matters easier but only more difficult. To this extent, then, we would argue that the CEPG have not understood the problem which confronts us.

On the other hand, their emphasis on the inflationary problems of devaluation accords very well with the argument of this book. It is indeed these inflationary problems which prevent devaluation, combined with suitable macroeconomic measures, from being sufficient to take us back to full employment. That being so, it is rather puzzling that the CEPG do not themselves put the problem of reconciling less unemployment and high profits with reasonably stable prices at the forefront of their discussions. In their March 1978 *Economic Review*, for example, they simply assume a certain rate of increase of wage settlements which is the same for all their different policy packages (i.e. a continuation of 'ortho-dox' policies, devaluation, and import restrictions). They nowhere point out that the behaviour of wages is the most important determinant of the level of employment in the long run. Perhaps they would regard any statement of this kind as profoundly mistaken. If so, in the writer's opinion they have failed to understand the essential nature of the problem of getting back to full employment.

(c) *Measures to increase the rate of growth of real disposable wages*

All governments since the war have wanted to increase productivity, and most people would accept that this is an important objective quite apart from its implications for restoring full employment. An excellent discussion of our productivity record in relation to that of other Western countries, of the reasons why it is so bad, and of recent government policies with respect to it is to be found in Cairncross, Kay and Silberston, 1977. Marksmen would accept that faster growing productivity (if it could be achieved) would tend to slow down inflation and permit higher employment, and would stress both this factor and also the possibility of tax cuts. The latter could continue over a long period if government expenditure were to grow more slowly than national expenditure. Tax cuts could also result for some time from the exploitation of North Sea Oil, or, for a still shorter time, from overseas borrowing. Monetarists would, however, not accept that any of these would reduce the natural level of unemployment. Indeed Phelps (1968, p. 703) has argued that faster growing productivity would probably increase it, by making greater demands on labour mobility. Hence no permanent reduction in unemployment could result from these measures, although there might, presumably, be some temporary alleviation in inflation while expectations adjusted to the faster growth in real wages. Militants would only regard the measures under this head as helpful in reducing unemployment in the long run through their effects on labour-using investment. In so far as this is stimulated (e.g. by measures which stimulate investment generally), *and by more than labour-saving investment*, the rate of growth of demand for labour is strengthened. This means that a higher share of wages in value-added can be permitted, since this will stimulate labour-saving investment and restore equilibrium between the growth of labour demand and supply. The higher share of wages will, in turn, reduce militancy, and this will permit a reduction in unemployment. It is only by this indirect route that unemployment is reduced, and it depends on the measures, whatever they are, strengthening the growth of labour demand. Whether they would do so seems uncertain—they might even have the opposite effect.

(d) *Increasing the rate of growth of employment in public services and/or reducing the rate of growth of the total labour force*

Governments have often stepped up public expenditure at times when they wanted to increase total demand, and this has led to rapidly growing public service employment as Bacon and Eltis (1978) have emphasized (see also Table 5.2). Although such measures have not had employment creation as their sole objective, this has been an objective which could become increasingly important as unemployment mounts. Employment can in principle be increased in this way, provided taxes are increased, without any increase in the government's budgetary deficit, borrowing requirement or growth in the money supply.[1] Hence some might feel that it was a simple and non-inflationary method of increasing employment. However, according to marksmen it must, in the long run, tend to increase unemployment, since it is precisely the reverse of the policies we have just considered under (c). It also follows from that discussion that monetarists must regard it as irrelevant in the long run. A militant, however, could accept that there might be a permanent reduction in registered unemployment. This is because the slower growth of the labour force in the 'marketed' sector would be consistent with a higher share of labour-saving investment in total investment. That, in turn, would allow there to be a higher share of wages in value-added, and that would reconcile the pressure to increase the share of wages with the need to keep the share constant in the long run at a lower level of unemployment. Hence we seem to have the complete spectrum of opinions here: more unemployment, no difference, and less unemployment.

Measures to reduce the rate of growth of the total labour force might include shortening hours of work, increasing the length and number of holidays, encouraging or insisting on earlier retirement, discouraging married women with children from seeking employment, lengthening education (including part-time education), and making it easier for those who prefer shorter hours to obtain part-time jobs (e.g. by introducing 4-hour shifts). Most, if not all, of these would probably slow down the rate of growth of the national product as conventionally measured, although whether they would involve a real loss of welfare is more doubtful—the reverse might be true for at least some. This is not, however, the point at issue. Would they help us to get back to full employment? If we accept the definition in Chapter 2, they might well do so, according to a militant's analysis (for reasons which are similar to those just given above), but probably not according to the other theories. There seems to be no reason why they should reduce the natural level of unemployment, and so, for a monetarist, the effect if any could only be temporary. A marksman, assuming that the target real wage is set in conventional terms and so does not include 'leisure' as income, and assuming also that it refers to income per family or per head of the population rather than per worker, would.regard such measures as positively harmful.

How can a mixer evaluate these different conclusions? It does seem important to reach some conclusion, since many of the measures mentioned have been advocated by the TUC (see *Trades Union Congress Economic Review 1978*, Chapter 1), and the government's temporary employment subsidy and other job-saving schemes are of a similar nature. They directly increase employment in the private, as well as the public, sector, but their effect on *total* employment, when *indirect* effects are allowed for, is the point at issue. The same might be said of proposals which have been made to reduce social security contributions, which are essentially a tax on employment. The simplest view is that of the monetarist: these measures cannot help since they do not influence the natural level of unemployment. As fast as we reduce unemployment by providing more public sector jobs, more subsidised (or less taxed) private sector ones, or by pushing more people into retirement, we have to increase unemployment somewhere else in order to prevent wages and prices from accelerating. So long as one believes that unemployment is indeed the policy of last resort which is used to counter inflation, then this simple view must be accorded respect. It may not contain the whole truth, but it must make one wonder whether the *net* gain to employment from measures such as these is at all sizeable. If one concludes that it is not, then one may also conclude that the cost of the measures themselves in terms of lower private consumption or investment may make them unattractive.[2] Of course, one may want to increase public sector employment at the expense of private consumption or investment for its own sake. That is another matter. The question here is different, namely, do we want to increase it, over and above the levels already determined on other grounds, purely in order to get a small increase in employment at the expense of a relatively large fall in private consumption and/or investment? The answer must then depend on the relative magnitudes involved.

In assessing these relative magnitudes, we must take account of the marksmen's and militants' points of view. If we believe that the rate of increase of real wages after tax is an important determinant of wage push, and if we believe that the level of unemployment is also important, then the measures are almost certainly harmful to employment. By aggravating inflation they will compel the government to increase, rather than reduce, unemployment. If, however, we believe that unemployment is not a significant factor in wage determination, then the simple monetarist argument becomes irrelevant. Increased employment in the public (or subsidised private) sector does not have to be matched by reduced employment elsewhere in order to prevent inflation accelerating. Consequently, for a pure marksman, much will turn on the real cost of the measures. If the jobs provided cost no more than the social security payments which otherwise would have to be paid, there is no increase in the tax burden and no extra inflationary pressure. However, for a pure marksman, would not tax cuts, or other measures to stimulate private demand, be better still?

So far as the militant's point of view is concerned, much depends on the reduction in the share of profits made possible by the smaller need for labour-using investment, and on how great an effect this smaller share of profits has on the rate of increase of wages. If these effects are all sizeable, then there could be an appreciable fall in unemployment.

The above discussion (like much else in this book) is merely an attempt to sort out the issues. No conclusion is possible without some estimates of the magnitudes of the effects involved, which we do not attempt to provide here.

(e) *Incomes policies*

By incomes policies we mean the kind of policies which have been used since the war in an attempt to slow down wage and price increases without increasing unemployment or deflating demand. We do not include the more radical policies which are discussed later on. Nevertheless, the range of policies included is very wide: from statutory policies which attempt to regulate virtually all wages and prices to 'toothless jawboning'. The subject is enormous, and much has been written about it, so that we cannot do more here than seek to outline the main ways in which such policies might hope to influence inflation—and so employment—and their main limitations and drawbacks.

There are two main ways in which the policies have worked, in so far as they have done so at all. First, they have influenced workers' and employers' expectations about 'the going rate' and about price increases (factors 1 and 2 in our list on p. 33). Secondly, they have reflected or influenced the attitude of the government and the media to wage increases (factor 9).

In order to have some influence in these ways, however, the policies have had to conform to certain characteristics which have, in the end, severely limited their effectiveness. Thus they have had to be rather simple and easily understood. The 'norm' may have been zero, or a flat rate increase for everyone, or an equal proportionate increase for everyone. Slightly more complicated variants have been tried (such as a combination of a flat rate and proportionate increase, with the added complication of an upper limit), but it has not been possible to base policy for any length of time on a complicated set of criteria. The reason is that this requires someone to interpret the application of the criteria in each particular case, and, since there are thousands of particular cases, that is not easy. Furthermore, even if it is attempted it leaves workers and employers with the suspicion that the norms are being 'bent' so as to allow bigger wage increases for those with a strong bargaining position. It is thus apt to degenerate into free collective bargaining, which means, in effect, no incomes policy at all. But if a complicated set of criteria cannot endure for long, neither can a very simple one. This is because circumstances keep changing, and so does the set of pay relativities which is appropriate. A simple incomes policy cannot cope with this, because the changes required are just too complicated to be grasped by any simple formula.

Secondly, the policies have all been temporary. They have generally been a response to a crisis of some kind. In these circumstances, it has been possible to appeal to the loyalty of workers and employers, who then agree to measures which they recognize as being in their collective interest but not in their private interest. It is difficult, however, to command that loyalty in peacetime for more than a year or two. It is not the function of trade union leaders, as they or their members see it, to hold down wages. It is not the function of employers, as businessmen see it, to hold down either wages or prices. Consequently, the incomes policies have either broken down or been brought to an end after a couple of years.

Thirdly, although there have been statutory policies, they have all rested on voluntary agreement by workers' representatives, including the TUC, who have therefore been able, in effect, to veto any particular scheme, or else to obtain concessions elsewhere in exchange for their agreement. There has been no effective sanction against a substantial and well organised group of workers determined to break the policy, at least so long as they have had the support of the TUC.

The fact that successive incomes policies have all broken down, both here and in other countries, shows that it is not easy to devise a permanent workable incomes policy in a free democratic country (they exist all right behind the Iron Curtain). The case against them has been brilliantly argued in Brittan and Lilley (1977). At the time of writing, there is still something remaining of the government's incomes policy, and indeed, given the size of the public sector, an incomes policy of a kind is inevitable. The government has to have some view as to what wage increases it will agree to in the public sector. In some future crisis there seems little doubt that we shall find ourselves back with a more all-embracing incomes policy, no doubt with some fresh twist, which will have some temporary effect. Past experience suggests, however, that we shall not be able to reconcile full employment and reasonable price stability in this way.

(f) *Monetarist policies*

These can be interpreted narrowly as meaning controlling the quantity of some defined money stock, or more widely as operating macroeconomic policy in such a way that the level of unemployment rises high enough to moderate wage increases. Naturally, one does not seek unemployment for its own sake, and so the attempt is made to influence expectations (factors 1 and 2) so as to bring down inflation with the minimum amount of unemployment. However, the fundamental factors which reduce the rate of wage increases are 3 and 4, those influencing the relationship between supply and demand for labour. Government policy at the time of writing appears to be relying on this for the most part, despite the fact that probably neither most members of the government nor most of its advisers are monetarists. The explanation for this probably is that the government feels it has been driven into a corner. It has not wanted to let unemployment increase, but it is unable to see anything else it can, in practice, do. While the IMF may have insisted in 1976–77 on a strict monetary and fiscal policy, it is likely that the government would have followed such a policy in any case (and it would have been even stricter without the IMF loan). Indeed, the decision at the end of October 1977 to let the pound float upwards suggests that the government was then still giving priority to reducing inflation over reducing unemployment in the short run. In so far as it was monetarist, it must have believed that the natural level of unemployment was 6 per cent or more (or else that inflation had to be brought down quickly).

Strict monetary policies alone can hardly be expected to restore full employment in the foreseeable future. If the latter means, say, 2.7 per cent unemployment (or thereabouts), while the natural level of unemployment is 6 (or even 4) per cent (see Chapter 4), this is obvious, if one is a monetarist. Hence monetarists must rely on other measures to reduce the natural level of unemployment, such as improving the efficiency of job centres, abandoning incomes policies which prevent relative wage changes, abandoning price controls, weakening the monopoly power of trades unions, reforming housing policy etc. Whether these would suffice is uncertain. However, monetarists would argue that there is nothing better that can be done. Militants and mixers would dispute this, and would favour some of the more radical policies mentioned below.

(g) *Measures proposed in the OECD Report 'Towards
    Full Employment and Price Stability'*

The OECD Report (McCracken *et. al.*, June 1977) was made
by a group of eight independent experts drawn from eight different
countries. Not surprisingly, it combines many different viewpoints
and theories (since, as is well-known, one economist is capable
of holding more than one opinion on any matter). It cannot,
therefore, be neatly classified into any of our three theoretical
positions. Its main recommendation is that governments should
cautiously expand demand while at the same time 'jaw-bone' as
hard as possible so as to reduce inflationary expectations. In this
way, it is believed, countries will be able to get back to full
employment (which is not precisely defined), reasonable price stability and growth.

> At the present time, the authorities should aim to steer demand
> along the relatively narrow path consistent with achieving a
> sustained recovery. The lower limit is set by the need for a
> rate of expansion sufficient to encourage a recovery in investment,
> both through spreading overhead costs and improving profit
> margins, and through creating expectations of the need for addi-
> tional capacity in the reasonably near future. The upper limit
> is set by the point at which a rapid increase in aggregate demand
> would re-ignite inflationary expectations. (p. 19)

This policy is similar to that described in (a) above which,
we said, would require James Bond's combination of luck and
skill to achieve. While it may be feasible for some countries,
is it for the UK? What if the 'lower limit' exceeds the 'upper
limit' so that the path ceases to exist (except in some metaphysical
negative sense!)? The Report is quite firm in stating that governments must not accommodate high rates of inflation. They must
set monetary and budgetary targets which make this impossible.
'We recognise that under unfavourable circumstances a policy of
non-accommodation based on the broad macroeconomic approach
we would prefer may still leave a situation in which either or
both inflation and unemployment remain at unacceptably high
levels. There may then be no alternative to policies which involve
more detailed intervention in the process of price and income
determination. It is our view, however, ... that, leaving aside

emergency situations, the costs of such policies have tended to be high in relation to any lasting benefits obtained, at least as far as the larger countries are concerned.' (p. 186) The Report is thus opposed to income and price controls, except as a last resort. It does, however, favour a variety of measures to influence expectations and attitudes, as well as attempts 'to reach a consensus on the need for higher profits and investment among the government, labour and management' (p. 25) and regular discussions between these parties on 'the general evolution of prices and wages to be aimed at over the coming year or so, consistent with achieving or maintaining high employment levels' (p. 26). Because of the difficulties of applying guidelines for individual wage and price decisions, the Report considers that 'fiscal or other devices designed to narrow the conflict, at the decentralised level at which wage and price decisions are actually taken, between the public interest and the self-interest of the parties directly concerned' deserve consideration (p. 217), and it instances the French 'conjunctural levy' as an example of one such device. This is a special refundable levy on larger companies on the amount by which their value-added per unit of input exceeds a predetermined norm. 'In other words, the levy is designed to penalise excessive increases in unit wages and/or profit margins.' This is one of the more radical proposals in the Report. Another is that governments should issue index-linked bonds. It makes many other proposals, similar to those already mentioned.

(h) *Measures proposed by the CBI in 'The future of pay determination', June 1977*

The CBI position appears to be that of a mixer. The discussion document cited stresses the shift in bargaining power which has occurred in favour of organized labour, and argues that the imbalance is especially great in the public sector. It rejects permanent controls as a solution, and believes that reliance on strict monetary and fiscal policies *alone* would probably lead to low profits, low investment, still extremely high unemployment, and loss in productivity.

'Before the 1970s it was believed by some that moderate deflation would produce a level of unemployment sufficient to restrain the growth of pay and as such was an alternative to direct intervention. More recent experience of high rates of pay increase during periods of high unemployment has suggested either that this relationship no longer exists or that the level of unemployment required to produce non-inflationary pay settlements would be intolerably high' (p. 13). The CBI therefore wants to combine strict monetary and fiscal policies (and cash limits in the public sector) with measures which will, in effect, reduce what we have called 'militancy', so that moderate wage increases can be reconciled with lower levels of unemployment.

The measures (briefly) are: the creation of a national consensus 'on the economic facts of life facing the nation and to communicate it to the country at large' (p. 21), perhaps through the NEDC, but also by involving Parliament (including the opposition parties) in some way or another; legislation on industrial relations with a view to righting the imbalance of bargaining power wherever there is wide acceptance of the need for such legislation; improvement of the system of collective bargaining in various ways so as to reduce the scope for leap-frogging (larger bargaining units in some cases so as to include groups of workers who regard each other as comparable, closer synchronization of bargaining, clear definition of which items (e.g. pay, fringe benefits, payments by results schemes) are to be negotiated at which levels (e.g. industry, company, plant)); closer coordination and solidarity of employers; further amalgamations of trades unions so as to reduce the scope for inter-union rivalry within bargaining units; improvement of the representativeness of trade union leaders, ratification of collective agreements by the membership, and a more formal framework for collective bargaining, procedures being more closely adhered to, with avoidance of unofficial and unconstitutional action; and various measures to promote a better knowledge of what is happening and understanding of the inter-relationships between pay, profits, prices, investment and jobs, including better information for and consultation with employees by companies, and participation agreements between them.

A monetarist might be inclined to dismiss most of this as pious hope—all the better information and understanding in the world will not alter the reality of supply and demand in the labour and goods markets. A militant, however, would believe (to repeat the quotation from Tobin) that 'there is an arbitrary, imitative component in wage settlements' which could be influenced by these measures. If it can be, the 'fly-wheel' of price and wage expectations will ensure that inflation slows down and remains low.

(i) *Various more radical measures*

In this last category we lump together a number of proposals made by different people, all of a fairly radical nature and all directed at reducing what we have called 'militancy' *without* increasing unemployment. The proposers have usually combined them with less radical measures already discussed (e.g. to fix targets for the growth in the money supply or the value of the national income as a guide to macroeconomic policy), and which we do not repeat, although this may make it appear that the persons concerned are more eccentric than they really are!

Meade (1975) proposes measures which would increase the responsiveness of both prices and wages to demand and supply conditions, thus making it easier to control inflation by macroeconomic policy without creating heavy unemployment. He lists several ways in which small firms could be encouraged relative to large ones (e.g. progressive taxes on employment, higher taxes on undistributed profits in excess of a certain absolute amount, institutions specialising in finance for small firms, changes in Company Law, control of mergers and take-overs, measures to lessen the economies of scale due to research and development) and also measures to promote competition between firms (control of restrictive practices, freer imports, taxes on advertising, abolition of commercial broadcasting, provision of consumer information by other means, such as *Which?*). He would like wage bargaining to be conducted on a firm-by-firm basis amongst a large number of small firms facing small unions. Recognizing that large firms and large unions will continue to exist, his next preference is for a national scheme of arbitration and, failing this, a system under which firms would be able to refer to a tribunal any wage claims which they considered exceeded a 'norm' laid down by the government. The tribunal's sole function would be to rule whether the claim did or did not in fact exceed the norm. If it did, and only then, certain financial sanctions would be brought into play against any workers striking in support of the claim (e.g. there might be loss of redundancy entitlements, supplementary benefits paid to strikers' families might have to be repaid subsequently or might be recovered from the trade unions concerned, strike pay might be taxed).

One might add, in the spirit of Meade's suggestions (though not in fact made in the work cited), that greater freedom for firms to invest abroad would reduce the monopoly power of labour

organizations. This need not necessarily imply complete freedom
for all capital movements, but could be confined to 'direct' investment by British companies abroad, and could be accompanied
by measures to ease repatriation of capital by foreign companies
and, possibly, to encourage investment by them.

Brittan (September 1976) has suggested that it might be possible
to reduce the danger that the threat of strike action will lead
to economic or political instability by offering workers different
kinds of labour contracts. Workers in 'essential' industries (i.e.
whose power to disrupt the economy is especially great) would
be offered complete job security in exchange for abandonment
of the right to strike. Their pay would have to be fixed by
comparison with workers elsewhere by some agreed means, and
it would be desirable to develop a market in the purchase and
sale of such jobs, so that, if workers had to be dismissed, compensation could be based on the market value of the job. Other workers
could retain the right to strike, but would not have job security.
Some workers might have no right to strike *and* no job security,
and some the right to strike *and* job security, but the main forms
of contract would probably be the first two. In the same paper
Brittan also suggests that strike threats should, if necessary, be
countered by contingency planning by the government to continue
essential services in the event of a strike, in this way reducing
the likelihood of a strike taking place.

Jay (1976) accepts the militancy theory, and is pessimistic about
the chances of reducing militancy by means other than the very
radical one of replacing private enterprise by worker cooperatives
(apart from some public utilities).

Our existing political economy is inherently unstable because
it insists upon a level of employment which is unattainable
without accelerating inflation under existing labour-market arrangements. There is no reasonable prospect of persuading the
electorate to accept the continuing level of unemployment which
would be associated with non-inflationary fiscal and monetary
policies under existing labour-market arrangements. Therefore
those arrangements must change in such a way as to remove
the general influence of collective bargaining and to enhance
the general efficiency of the labour market .... The general
influence of collective bargaining can only be removed by offering
working people an alternative and better protection than national

trade unions can offer. The only potentially acceptable alternative is a change in Company Law which gives ownership and ultimate control of enterprises to the people employed by them. They would then have to sink or swim in the market environment. Inflation would subside. Employment would be high. The sovereignty of the consumer would be assured. The 'hidden hand' would continue its benign dispositions. The corporate state and its handmaiden, the national trade union, and the bureaucracy of the mixed economy, would wither away. The democracy of the ballot-box, of the market-place, and of the work-place would prevail over the otherwise impossible power of giant organisations, most particularly of government itself. It is at least an alternative to the anarchy followed by the strong-man to which present arrangements are inexorably leading us. (pp. 33, 34).

8 A model of inflation and unemployment

This chapter, addressed in the main to economists, describes a model which the writer has found useful in analysing both the UK's experience of unemployment and inflation since the war and the policy issues that confront us. It brings together many of the ideas from the preceding chapters and shows how they are inter-related. It allows for disequilibrium as well as dynamic equilibrium, which is essential in any useful attempt to describe what has happened, or to trace the long-term consequences of different policies, or to understand the implications of the different theories—militant, monetarist, or marksman—we have considered. Although it is a great simplification of reality, and cannot claim to fit it precisely nor to explain everything, it is still quite a complicated scheme of thought. Fortunately, it lends itself well to diagrammatic representation, but the reader must be prepared to consider each of the three basic diagrams carefully and to grasp their inter-relationships. We consider the full-employment era first, then the period of rising unemployment 1966–74, and finally the recession years since 1974, employing the same three basic diagrams A, B and C to analyse the situation in each of these periods.

THE FULL EMPLOYMENT ERA, 1948–66

In Fig. 8.1 we use the three basic diagrams to illustrate the full employment era. We explain each in turn, working from the top downwards.

FIG. 8.1   *Model to explain inflation and unemployment, 1948–66*

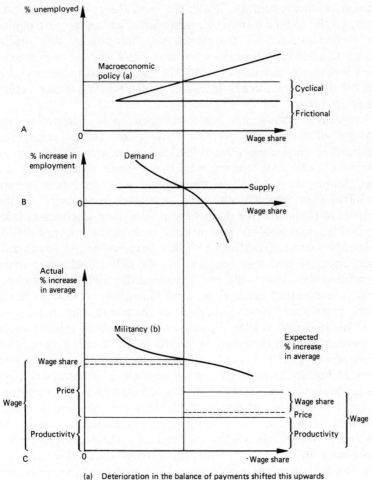

(a)   Deterioration in the balance of payments shifted this upwards
(b)   Lower unemployment shifted this upwards & rightwards

All three diagrams measure the same thing along the horizontal axis: the share of income from employment in total income (value-added) generated in what is best described as the 'marketed sector' of the economy. In what follows, we refer to this as 'the share of wages' for short. By 'marketed sector' we mean roughly the same as Bacon and Eltis (1978), that is, we exclude public adminis-'tration, defence, education, health etc. from the gross domestic product, GDP, and take the remainder. Since we are not attempting an econometric test of the model, we shall not be very precise about its scope (for example, whether imputed rents of owner-occupied houses are included or not). For the most part, we rely only on the data given already in earlier tables, which are not exactly what are needed.

Diagram A shows how macro-economic policy determines the *average* share of wages over the trade cycle. The government is assumed to choose an average level of unemployment (shown on the vertical axis, and referring here to the whole economy and not just the marketed sector) in the light of its objectives in regard to inflation or, alternatively, as it feels itself constrained by the balance of payments. We discuss the first of these alternatives later on making use of ideas put forward by Nordhaus (April 1975).

It is the second alternative which best describes the 1948–66 experience, since the exchange rate *vis-à-vis* the dollar (and many other currencies) was fixed throughout this period. Nor did the government wish to use import controls or tariff changes to correct a deficit in the balance of payments for most of the period. Import controls were last tightened in 1951–52, and were subsequently relaxed, more or less disappearing altogether by the late 1950's. Tariffs were reduced in successive GATT rounds, with only one temporary reversal in 1964. Hence, the government's main response to a balance of payments deficit was restriction of demand through fiscal and monetary policy. This implied a certain average level of cyclical unemployment, and that, in turn, implied a particular average share of wages. As diagram A shows, the higher the level of cyclical unemployment, the greater the share of wages. Since employment fluctuated by less than output, profits were squeezed in a recession, and the deeper the average recession the smaller was the average share of profits, or the greater that of wages.

Only frictional and cyclical unemployment are shown in Diagram A, as it is assumed that structural unemployment was zero throughout the period. In effect, as was explained in Chapter 2, structural unemployment in the period is included with frictional, and our subsequent analysis is confined to *additional* structural unemployment, over and above the level existing in 1948–66.

Diagram B shows how the rates of *growth* of the demand for

and supply of labour in the 'marketed sector', measured along the vertical axis, are related to the share of wages. The rate of growth of the supply of labour is assumed to be independent of the share of wages, being determined by demographic, social and political factors. These control both the rate of growth of the total labour force and that of employment in the 'non-marketed sector'. As may be seen from Table 5.2, there was a small positive rate of growth of rather less than 1 per cent per annum in total civilian employment excluding 'public services' from 1948–66. As unemployment changed little, this was also the rate of growth of the labour supply to the 'marketed sector'.

The rate of growth of the demand for labour by the 'marketed sector' is shown as falling the higher is the share of wages. This conforms with the theory of labour-using and labour-saving investment described in chapter 5. A higher share of wages (and so lower share of profits) is assumed to reduce total investment, and especially labour-using investment.

Diagram B shows that, at the average share of wages determined in Diagram A, the growth in demand for labour matched the growth in supply. This implies that there was no change in structural unemployment from 1948–66. The main evidence for this is the stability in the unemployment/vacancies relationship as shown in Figs. 2.1 and 2.2. It was only *after* 1966, as we saw in Chapter 2, that there appeared to be a rightward shift in the curve relating unemployment to vacancies, which we explained (partly) in terms of increasing structural unemployment.

Diagram C shows how the average rate of wage increases is related to the share of wages. This is the most complex of our three diagrams. In explaining it, we start with the viewpoint of a 'mixer' who believes that the theories of monetarists, militants and marksmen each contain part of the truth. Subsequently, we show how each of these theories in their pure forms would appear.

A mixer believes that all the nine factors listed on p. 33 influence the rate of wage increases. However, it is not possible to show the effect of all of these in Diagram C, and we have chosen to show the share of wages (which relates to factors 6 and 7). The greater this is, given all the other factors, the smaller is the rate of increase in wages, for the reasons discussed in Chapter 4. Hence the 'militancy' curve, as we have called it, slopes downwards to the right. All the other factors must then shift the curve. In particular, as the note in the Diagram states, lower unemployment (factors

3 & 4), shifts the curve upwards and rightwards. This would also be true of a lower cost of being on strike (factor 8) and a more favourable attitude to wage increases on the part of the government or the media (factor 9). This still leaves us with expectations about wage and price increases (factors 1 and 2) and target real wage increases (factor 5). How can their influence be shown?

The crucial questions, as we shall presently see, are whether wage increases are such as to increase or decrease the share of wages, and how expectations are borne out in practice. The expectations we are mainly concerned with are those of workers and trade union leaders, but we do not distinguish sharply between these and the expectations of employers. Diagram C is divided into two parts. On the right, we show *expected* percentage changes in *average* productivity, prices and the share of wages. To a first approximation, the sum of these three percentage changes equals the expected percentage change in *average* wages. On the left, we show the *actual* percentage changes in average productivity, prices and the share of wages, which approximately sum to the actual percentage change in average wages.

We must emphasize that both the expected and actual changes refer to *averages*. Thus, for example, we have shown the expected average increase in wages as being less than the actual average increase. This is because we think it likely that, at the time of each wage settlement, when both parties knew what the relevant increase in wages was for that particular settlement, they probably had in mind an expected rate of increase in average wages which was below the actual average increase. So in most settlements, wage earners may have thought that they were going to do better than the average, although it turned out, of course, that on average wage earners cannot do better than average. Exactly how the different components of the expected and actual wage change were related to each other is uncertain. We have assumed, in Diagram C, that only a very small price increase was expected and that the expected rate of growth of productivity was the same as the actual, but this is guesswork. For simplicity, we have assumed that the expected and actual increases in average productivity were the same in 1948–66.

If we ignore, for the present, questions of taxation, or the difference between the 'product wage' and the wage in terms of purchasing power over consumption goods, we can also show changes in expected and actual *real* wages in Diagram C. The percentage increase in real wages is, approximately, the percentage increase in money wages less the percentage increase in prices. Alternatively, it is the sum of the percentage increases in productivity and in the share of wages. Diagram C assumes that the expected increase in real wages in 1948–66 was greater than the actual increase.

We are now able to show how changes in expectations (factors 1 and 2) and in the target real wage increase (factor 5) affect actual wage increases. It is convenient to consider the points of view of monetarists, militants and marksmen separately, before attempting to synthesise them.

A monetarist who believed that supply and demand in the labour market (i.e. factors 3 and 4) were the most important accelerating or braking factors, and who discounted the importance of the share of wages (factors 6 and 7), would replace the downward sloping 'militancy' curve in Diagram C by a horizontal line whose position would be determined by the level of unemployment (as well as by the other factors which we mentioned in Chapter 4 as determining the natural level of unemployment). Any increase in the expected rate of change of prices would result in an (at least) equal increase in the rate of change of wages, and the same would be true of any increase in the expected rate of change of productivity. If unemployment were at its natural level, by definition the rate of wage increases would lead to neither accelerating nor decelerating wage or price increases. For this to be so, in the long run, the share of wages must be constant. The 'militancy' curve would then coincide with the expected price line (i.e. the broken line on the right-hand side of Diagram C) which would also coincide with the actual price line; and wage increases would equal the sum of expected and actual price and productivity increases. It is clear from this that any change in these must be matched by equal changes in wages, unless such changes in some way affect the natural level of unemployment. The monetarist position seems to be that any such effects are likely, if they exist at all, to be in the direction of increasing the natural level.

Thus Friedman (1977), after reviewing evidence showing that higher levels of unemployment have been accompanied by faster rates of inflation in several countries, argues that there may well be a positively sloped Phillips Curve in the long run. This would result from greater instability of inflation which typically accompanies faster average inflation, and from the lower efficiency of the market system under these conditions, as well as the tendency for governments to attempt to control prices. In the *very* long run, the system would probably adapt to all of these, and then unemployment would revert to its natural level, and there would be a vertical Phillips Curve once more. However, this period of adaptation might take several decades. Phelps (1968, p. 703) has argued that faster growing productivity would probably increase the natural level of unemployment, by making greater demands on labour mobility. The implication of a rise in the natural level of unemployment is that the (horizontal) militancy curve must rise, since at any given level of unemployment, and given expectations, wage increases must be faster. So much for the monetarist position.

The militant position differs inasmuch as it allows the militancy curve to slope downwards to the right, as drawn. But the height of the curve above the expected price line would be (as for some monetarists) more or less independent of the magnitude of expected price or productivity changes. Thus, as for some monetarists, any increase in the expected rate of change of prices would result in an equal increase in the rate of change of wages, and the same would be true of any increase in the expected rate of change of productivity. This result follows from the militant view that workers press for wage increases until they meet with strong resistance. In so far as employers expected prices or productivity to grow faster, their resistance to wage increases would be *pro tanto* weakened. Militants would probably not, however, go so far as some monetarists in arguing that the militancy curve would be shifted upwards (with respect to the expected price line) by faster expected price or productivity increases. Indeed, insofar as workers or their leaders showed greater restraint *because* of faster inflation (as some militants allege), the militancy curve would be shifted downwards. Some militants may object that this analysis is unrealistic in assuming that workers formulate explicit expectations about changes in prices or productivity. We deal with this objection below.

Marksmen, like monetarists, would require a horizontal militancy curve (since wage increases would be independent of the wage share). This curve's height above the expected price line would depend on the target real wage increase and would be independent of the position of that line, so that any increase in the expected rate of change of prices would result in an equal increase in the rate of change of wages. This must be so if workers are aiming at a particular *real* wage increase. However, the effect of expected productivity change is radically different. Unlike both monetarists and militants, marksmen would require the militancy curve to fall (with respect to the expected price line) by the amount of any expected increase in the rate of change of productivity. Consequently, for a given rate of price increase, faster growth in productivity would reduce the rate of increase in the share of wages *pro tanto*, instead of (as with monetarists and militants) leaving it broadly speaking unchanged. The same would be true of any other change enabling real disposable wages to grow faster without putting pressure on prices or profit margins. Thus improvements in the terms of trade (resulting in a slower rise in consumer prices than in the price of output), or cuts in government expenditure (resulting in cuts in direct or indirect taxes) would all have similar effects, whereas for monetarists and militants there would be no such effects.

A synthesis of these views would presumably assume that any change in expected price increases would be more or less fully reflected in money wage increases, but might allow that faster growth in productivity (or the other factors just mentioned) would exert some dampening effect.

Our three diagrams illustrate the *average* position in 1948–66. In fact, by comparison with preceding or succeeding years, 1948–66 was in many respects a very stable period, so that the average position in each of our diagrams provides quite a good representation of the whole of it. There is nothing inconsistent with long-term dynamic equilibrium in either Diagram A or B. It is in Diagram C that the trouble is revealed. As drawn, the expected rates of increase of both wages and prices are much below the actual rates, and clearly this is not compatible with long-term equilibrium. Eventually, expectations must adjust to experience.

This way of putting it accords well with the monetarist analysis given in Chapter 4, but we can also interpret Brown's and Goldthorpe's non-monetarist analysis so as to accord with it as well. The actual money wage increases looked big if one related them to pre-war norms, and this is shown in Diagram C by the big increase in the share of wages which they would have implied if prices had been as stable as pre-war. However, in practice, as is shown on the left-hand side of the diagram, since prices were rising much faster than pre-war, the increase in the share of wages was very small. Hence the dangerous consequences (in terms of bankruptcies and unemployment) which would have followed in a more stable price situation did not, in fact, materialise. As this fact gradually sank home, and as younger men with different norms replaced older ones, larger wage increases were demanded and conceded. This could be shown in Diagram C by shifting the expected price line upwards (to show that the new norm was a situation in which larger wage increases were compatible with no bankruptcies or unemployment) which, in turn, shifts up the rate of actual wage increases by about the same amount. We have spelled all this out at some length to meet the objection that workers do not formulate any explicit price or productivity expectations, whereas our diagram seems to imply that they do. In fact, we do not need to assume that they do. All that we assume is that norms for wage increases are established, and are adjusted upwards until it is felt to be dangerous to push them up any more. In 1948–66 it apparently took a long time before the upward adjustment got under way, and it was thanks to this that we enjoyed full employment for so long.

A marksman might also accept Diagram C, believing that workers' price expectations, conditioned by pre-war experience, deceived them into thinking that they were achieving larger real wage increases than they did. Stability was lost once price expectations started adjusting upwards. However, some marksmen might prefer to pin responsibility for the breakdown, not on changing expectations, but on smaller real wage increases after tax following the return of a Labour Government in 1964. As Table 4.1 shows, for a typical wage-earner, real earnings after tax increased on average by only some 0.7 per cent per annum from 1964 to 1969. It was this very slow rate of real increase which forced money wages upwards—the reverse of the process described above in which (for a marksman) faster growing productivity (or similar factors) damps down money wage increases. Hence, while a monetarist or militant would regard a breakdown as inevitable sooner or later (and the surprising fact was how late it was), a marksman might consider that a breakdown could have been avoided altogether if total output had grown faster or government expenditure more slowly, thus allowing real wages after tax to grow faster.

Was full employment achieved only by deception? This is the monetarist view. Unemployment can only be held below its natural level by fooling people, and in 1948–66 they were fooled for a long time into holding wage and price expectations which did not correspond with reality. We have also seen that both militants and marksmen might concur with this conclusion, despite reaching it by different routes. However, as we have also seen, *some* marksmen might not agree. Furthermore, there is an important sense in which, if one adopts the militant viewpoint, one might reject the conclusion that workers' leaders were fooled in 1948–66. They were, on the contrary, quite right in believing that larger money wage increases were dangerous. The danger was that they would lead to faster inflation and higher unemployment, which is precisely what has happened. Unfortunately, it has taken a long time for this to become apparent to the new generation of leaders.

RISING UNEMPLOYMENT, 1966–74

From late 1967 until early 1971, macroeconomic policy was restrictive (see McCracken et al., June 1977, p. 91). The pound was devalued in November 1967, and the government was determined to make the devaluation effective. A large surplus on the balance of payments was achieved, but this was welcomed since it enabled foreign debts to be repaid. Restriction continued under the Conservative Government elected in 1970, and was not reversed until 1971. Thereafter, the floating of the exchange rate meant that domestic inflation rather than the balance of payments became the main constraint on macroeconomic policy. In terms of Diagram A, this meant that the government chose the average share of wages and average cyclical unemployment by reference to the rate of inflation rather than by reference to the state of the balance of payments.

We have illustrated the average situation in Diagram A of Fig. 8.2. The vertical share of wages line is further to the right, so that both the share of wages and cyclical unemployment are greater than in the full-employment era. Total unemployment is higher for two additional reasons: higher frictional unemployment for reasons discussed in Chapter 2, and some structural unemployment.

The latter grew throughout the period, as shown in Diagram B. There was actually a fall in the labour supply to the marketed sector, as may be seen from Table 5.2, so that the rate of growth of supply became negative. But the rate of growth of demand was evidently even more negative, as structural unemployment increased. This low rate of growth of demand was due, we have argued, to the switch from labour-using to labour-saving investment induced by the rise in the share of wages.

Coming finally to Diagram C, we have shown the rate of growth of productivity continuing at much the same rate as in the full employment era. The big change was the increase in the expected rate of growth of wages and prices, leading to a faster increase

Fig. 8.2   *Model to explain inflation and unemployment, 1966–74*

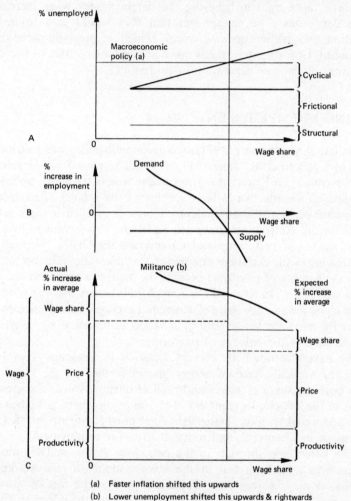

(a)   Faster inflation shifted this upwards
(b)   Lower unemployment shifted this upwards & rightwards

in the actual rate of growth of wages. Unemployment would (according to a mixer) have shifted the militancy curve downwards with respect to the expected price line, thus reducing the actual increase in wages. The latter should also have been reduced by the move rightwards along the militancy curve as the share of wages increased. However, these dampening factors may have been offset by other factors tending to increase militancy. There was the lowering of the tax threshold, in real terms, and, towards the end of the period, the very big worsening in the terms of trade which lowered the purchasing power over consumption goods of a given product wage. There was the new generation of more militant workers and their leaders, with very different experiences to guide them. At all events, there seems to have been an increase in militancy to judge by the fact that the number of working days lost due to industrial disputes increased markedly after 1967. In view of this, we have assumed in the diagram that the height of the militancy curve above the expected price line (at the actual share of wages) was about the same as in 1948–66. There was a faster actual increase in the share of wages in manufacturing industry (see Table 5.3). If this was true of the marketed sector generally, as is assumed in the diagram, it follows that the actual and expected price increases were closer together than in 1948–66. This seems plausible, the implication being that expectations were adjusting upwards more quickly.

It is clear from Diagrams B and C that 1966–74 was a period of dynamic disequilibrium. Structural unemployment was growing and inflation was accelerating.

RECESSION YEARS, 1974–77

This period is really too short to fit comfortably into our analysis, which is designed to portray the average position over one or more trade cycles. We have therefore not illustrated it in any figure. Its main features, were we to do so, would be: a further shift to the right of the share of wages line accompanying still higher cyclical unemployment; probably more frictional unemployment; a continuing deficiency of labour-using investment leading to further growth in structural unemployment; faster price increases resulting in faster wage increases, partially offset by a fall in the militancy curve, due to higher unemployment, together with a move downwards along it, due to the higher share of wages. The above is in terms of the average for the period compared with the average for 1966–74. However, within the period there was a significant turnround from accelerating to decelerating wage and price increases and, by the end of it, unemployment had apparently stopped growing. The rise in the share of wages had reduced profits to very low levels indeed, and there was a fall in militancy probably due to the much higher level of unemployment, to an attitude on the part of the government and the media which was more hostile to wage and price increases, with trade union leaders and their members sharing in this as well. There was a general revulsion from the 30 per cent wage increases and 25 per cent price increases of 1974–75. The TUC's wage guidelines were followed, even though they led to falling real wages and a recovery in profits. A variety of special government measures helped to stop unemployment growing (see chapter 2).

AN ANALYSIS OF THE LONG-TERM EFFECTS OF DIFFERENT POLICIES

In order to perceive the long-term effects of the different policies described in Chapter 7, we need to bring out the interrelationships between our three basic diagrams. It is also convenient to present the analysis in terms of a comparison of different long-term dynamic equilibrium positions, since we can, in this way, show the full long-term effects of the different policies. It is quite likely that unemployment and inflation will never settle down to steady levels, even when we average them across the trade cycle. There are so many lags in the system that events are likely to follow a cyclical course, with periods of higher and lower unemployment, and of faster and slower inflation. Nevertheless, the essential points can most easily be grasped by considering long-term dynamic equilibrium.

The conditions for such an equilibrium are also (some of) the conditions for maintaining full employment in the long-run, so that they are undoubtedly important. They may be listed in order of our three basic diagrams as follows.

(i) The government must feel satisfied with the combination of inflation (we shall assume throughout that there is a floating exchange rate, so that it is inflation, rather than the balance of payments, which constrains the government's macroeconomic policy) and unemployment which has been achieved. We do not mean that the government is satisfied in some absolute sense with the levels achieved. It may be absolutely dissatisfied. All we mean is that, given all the other factors in the situation, the government does not want to use macro-economic policy

to select, for example, a lower average level of cyclical unemployment, because it considers that the resulting additional
inflation would not be worthwhile.

(ii) The share of wages (and hence of profits) must make the
amount and composition of investment, as between labour-
using and labour-saving, such as to cause the growth of the
demand for labour in the marketed sector to match the growth
of supply. In short, structural unemployment must be constant,
so that in Diagram B the demand and supply curves intersect
each other and the vertical share of wages line at the same
point.

(iii) The rate of increase of wages must approximately equal the
sum of the rates of growth of prices and productivity, so
that there is no change in the share of wages. Furthermore,
price and productivity expectations must correspond to reality.
Hence, in Diagram C, the militancy curve must intersect the
expected price line and the vertical share of wages line at
the same point, and the actual and expected price lines must
coincide.

With these conditions fulfilled, unemployment, the share of wages,
and the rate of inflation will all be constant.

THE EFFECTS OF MACROECONOMIC POLICY

Policy can choose between different long-term equilibrium positions.
We confine ourselves, to begin with, to macroeconomic policy. This
enables us to see its limitations, and clears the way for a consideration
of other policies which seek to influence various factors which macroeconomic policy takes as given.

We continue our analysis with the aid of Fig. 8.3. Inflation and
unemployment are measured along the axes, and, as in Nordhaus
(April, 1975), the government is assumed to select different combinations of these through its macroeconomic policy. The curved lines
each show those combinations between which the government is
indifferent, and are similar to contour lines on a map. Unlike Nordhaus, we have assumed that the government believes that some
positive rate of inflation combined with a positive level of unemployment would be best, if it could be achieved, and this is shown
by point B_1. Given downward rigidity in some prices (including

FIG. 8.3   *Policy choices between inflation and unemployment*

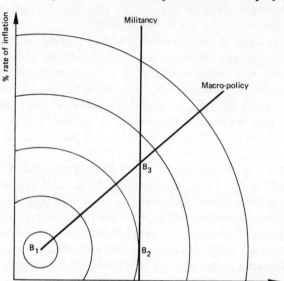

the price of labour), a low rate of inflation may be better than no inflation at all. Likewise, some frictional and, on average, cyclical unemployment may be necessary in a free economy. B_1 is then the top of the hill, and all other combinations of unemployment and inflation are inferior. To the North-East, for example, we are crossing lower and lower (i.e. less preferred) contour lines.

The line labelled 'macro-policy' shows the direction in which the government will choose to go if it is forced to depart from B_1. This is similar to the income-expenditure line in the theory of consumer choice. Its position is determined by the trade-off between inflation and unemployment which the government believes confronts it. As the line is drawn in Fig. 8.3, the government believes that there is a trade-off, which is measured by the slope of the indifference curves at their intersection with the macro-policy line.

There may, however, in reality be no trade-off. This possibility is illustrated by the vertical 'militancy' line in Fig. 8.3, which is derived from Diagram B and C in the following way. Let us assume that macroeconomic policy cannot affect the rate of growth of the demand for labour in the long run, apart from its effects on the share of wages. It could be argued that there are three other ways in which it could do so. First, by increasing the pressure of demand, it could encourage investment, especially of a capacity-increasing and labour-using kind. This may be so, but it is already adequately allowed for in Diagram B, since the rate of growth of the demand for labour is indeed assumed to depend on the average share of wages and cyclical unemployment, which will both vary in line with changes in the pressure of demand. Secondly, by moving the economy from a lower to a higher degree of capacity utilisation, macroeconomic policy could secure temporarily a faster rate of growth. This might suffice, however, to alter businessmen's expectations about the rate of growth of demand and to encourage them to undertake more labour-using investment. This pump-priming does seem to be a real possibility, even if difficult to bring off in practice. It cannot easily be allowed for in our diagrammatic analysis, however, so we postpone consideration of it until later. Thirdly, it could be argued that macro-economic policy can influence (real) interest rates. However, even if we suppose that it can, which some would deny, it is not clear that this would have much, or any, effect on the rate of growth of the demand for labour. Both labour-using and labour-saving invest-ment would be affected, but it is not clear that one would be more affected than the other, so that the net effect on the rate of growth of the demand for labour might be small. If this is granted, then, apart from the second possibility referred to above, to which we return subsequently, condition (ii) for long-term equilibrium implies that the share of wages is determined in Diagram B. Only one share of wages will make the demand for labour grow as fast as the supply, and that share of wages will have to rule in the long-run.

Turning now to Diagram C, and assuming that all the other factors which determine militancy are given, apart from the level of unemployment, we can see that, subject to the proviso given below, there is only one level of unemployment which will set the militancy curve at the right level to intersect the expected price line at zero change in the share of wages, as required by condition (iii). The proviso is that changes in the expected rates of increase of prices or productivity lead to equal changes in the rate of wage increases. So long as that is true, then the position of the militancy curve with respect to the expected price line does not depend on the expected rate of increase of prices or productivity. Assuming that is so for the moment, it follows that there is only one level of unemployment consistent with long-run dynamic equilibrium, and this is similar to the monetarists' natural level. That level is, however, and granted our proviso, consistent with any rate of inflation. Hence, on these assumptions, the real trade-off which confronts the government is shown by the vertical militancy line in Fig. 8.3, that is, there is no trade-off at all in the long-run.

We will change some of these assumptions presently, but let us first pursue their implications a little further. If the government behaves in the way described by the macro-policy line in Fig. 8.3, it will eventually reach point B_3. This is very much worse than B_1, with inflation and unemployment both much higher. It is also worse than the point it could reach were it to take a long-term view and to appreciate the true nature of the choices confronting it (given our assumptions). It cannot reduce unemployment in the long-run (through macroeconomic policy, that is) but it can reduce inflation. As the figure shows, its best feasible position, taking a long-term view and using macroeconomic policy as its only weapon, would be B_2.

Let us now see how these conclusions might be altered by different assumptions about the determinants of wages. A monetarist would not want to alter them very much. He would find Diagram B unnecessary, since he would not regard the share of wages as playing an independant part in wage determination, and would therefore not need Diagram B to fix the share of wages in the long run. There would be a unique level of unemployment in Diagram C at which the militancy curve (a horizontal line) would coincide with the expected price line, giving a constant wage share. This unique level would then produce the vertical militancy line, corresponding to the vertical Phillips curve, in Fig. 8.3. However, while this analysis reaches the same conclusion so far as macroeconomic policy is concerned, it fails to reveal some policy options. For, if our earlier (mixer) analysis is correct, policies which shift either the demand or supply curves of labour in Diagram B will change the long-term equilibrium share of wages. By doing so, they will also change the long-term equilibrium level of unemployment, that is, they will shift the vertical militancy line in Fig. 8.3 rightwards or leftwards. Any policy which, for example, succeeds in reducing the rate of growth of the supply of labour (and we considered several in chapter 7), will increase the equilibrium share of wages. This will permit a higher militancy curve in Diagram C, which, in turn, permits a lower equilibrium level of unemployment, and so shifts the vertical militancy line leftwards in Fig. 8.3. Thus there is a whole set of policies which, in monetarist terms, will reduce the natural level of unemployment but to which, so far as the writer is aware, monetarists have not drawn attention.

As was mentioned earlier, some monetarists have argued that faster price or productivity increases might increase the natural level of unemployment. If we ignore productivity increases, as being largely outside the scope of macroeconomic policy, then the implication of this view for our analysis is that the militancy line in Fig. 8.3 should slope upwards to the right. This means that a short-sighted, or misguided, macroeconomic policy would result in both more unemployment and more inflation than a farsighted one.

Turning now to the militants' viewpoint, let us first consider one according to which changes in expected prices in the long-run are fully reflected in wage increases, and unemployment has no effect at all. The share of wages does affect the rate of wage increases (i.e. there is a downward slope to the militancy line in Diagram C), but, in the long-run, that share is determined in Diagram B. It would only be chance that made that share consistent with a constant rate of inflation in Diagram C. Consequently, there is no long-term militancy line in Fig. 8.3. The government is then confronted with the following choice. It can either select the optimum level of unemployment (that at B_1 in the chart) by means of its macroeconomic policy, and tackle inflation with other weapons; or else it can select the optimum rate of inflation (again, at B_1 in the chart) by means of its macroeconomic policy, and tackle unemployment with other weapons. Its influence on either unemployment or inflation is through its determination of the share of wages. By setting the share sufficiently low it can eventually eliminate structural unemployment and also keep average cyclical unemployment at the required level. This may result in accelerating inflation, which has to be tackled with other weapons. Alternatively, by setting the share sufficiently high (so that enough firms are threatened by bankruptcy, or go bankrupt), it can keep inflation at the required rate. This may result in growing unemployment, which has to be tackled with other weapons.

Next, we consider the militant view that faster inflation itself shifts the militancy curve downwards. This alters matters, since there is now a determinate long-run equilibrium once more. A sufficient rate of inflation will lower the militancy curve in Diagram C so that it cuts the expected price line at the equilibrium share of wages as determined in Diagram B. We might call this the 'natural rate of inflation', bearing in mind that it may change from time to time, and could become greater and greater if successively larger doses of inflation were required to reduce militancy to the required level (this seems quite plausible—but might not a similar argument be applied to the natural level of unemployment?). In Fig. 8.3 we should then draw a *horizontal* militancy line, indicating that the rate of inflation would not, in the long run, be controlled by macroeconomic policy. The implication would be that macroeconomic policy should select the level of unemployment corresponding to B_1, and the government should tackle inflation with other weapons.

Next, we consider the marksman point of view. This can be done very briefly. If the long-term growth of productivity and of other factors influencing the growth of real wages (such as the rate of growth of government expenditure), are deemed to be outside the scope of macroeconomic policy, then a pure marksman would have to say that the latter could not control the rate of inflation. The implication would seem to be that macroeconomic policy should select the optimum level of unemployment, and the government should tackle inflation with other weapons.

Finally, let us try to arrive at a synthesis of these different viewpoints, but excluding that of the marksman since it is irrelevant on our interpretation of 'macroeconomic policy'. If we accept that both unemployment and the share of wages influence the rate of wage increases, and if we also accept the militant view that faster inflation is likely to reduce militancy (instead of the opposite conclusion of some monetarists), then we are left with a militancy line in Fig. 8.3 that slopes upwards to the *left*. This would imply that there was a long run trade-off between inflation and unemployment. Assuming that the line was much steeper than the short-run trade-off of the ordinary Phillips curve, our original conclusion would not be much affected. A short-sighted government would still end up with more inflation than a farsighted one. However, it would now end up with somewhat less unemployment, though perhaps not very much.

OTHER POLICIES

Our analysis thus far has related to the long-term effects of macroeconomic policy in a situation in which there is a floating exchange rate. We have thus dealt with policy (a) in Chapter 7. Policy (b) is the same as (a), but with import restrictions being used to maintain the exchange rate at a higher level than would otherwise be possible. Our diagrams do not enable us to add anything to what was said about this alternative in Chapter 7. Let us now run through the remaining policies in that chapter.

(c) *Increase the rate of growth of real disposable wages.*

A crucial issue here is whether militancy is reduced by this. A marksman would say that it would be. If so, the militancy curve in Fig. 8.3 is shifted leftwards, and unemployment falls as well as inflation. Even if this were not the case, however, there might be another effect through Diagram B. If faster productivity growth resulted from measures which increased labour-using more than labour-saving investment, the growth of demand for labour would accelerate, with similar results to those of pump-priming. Hence the militancy curve in Fig. 8.3 would, again, be shifted leftwards, reducing both unemployment and inflation. Whether this is at all likely, however, is by no means clear.

(d) *Increase the rate of growth of employment in public services and/or reduce the rate of growth of the total labour force.*

Both these policies reduce the rate of growth of the supply of labour to the marketed sector. Consequently, in Diagram B they shift the equilibrium wage share to the right, and this has the same effect as in pump-priming, that is, unemployment falls and inflation does as well. However, their effect on the rate of growth of real disposable wages is precisely the opposite of (c). Hence, if one is a marksman one might take the view that the resulting increase in militancy would undo, or even outweigh, the first effects, so that the net result could be to increase both unemployment and inflation.

(e) *Incomes Policies.*

We can interpret these as attempts to reduce militancy. In so far as they are successful, they will reduce both unemployment and inflation.

(f) *Monetarist Policies.*

A monetarist might accept Fig. 8.3, but not all the reasoning behind it. He might then say that the only constructive policy was to reduce what we have called 'frictional' unemployment, since this does not bear on wage and price increases. Apart from this, the position of the vertical militancy curve in Fig. 8.3, which corresponds to the vertical long-run Phillips curve, could not be altered, but inflation could be reduced to an optimum level by a suitable shift in the macro-policy curve.

(g) *OECD Report.*

The report's main recommendation can be interpreted as being 'pump-priming'. Demand should be gently expanded so as to encourage investment, but not so much as to rekindle inflation. One wants to engineer a rightward shift of the rate of growth of demand for labour in Diagram B. Apart from that, the most radical proposal in the report—a (cautious) recommendation that taxes on wage and profit increases should be considered—can be regarded as an attempt to reduce militancy by making it financially less attractive. If it succeeded, it would then reduce both unemployment and inflation.

(h) *CBI Discussion Paper.*

Again, a number of measures are proposed which, if successful, would reduce militancy and so, in Fig. 8.3, reduce both unemployment and inflation.

(i) *Various more radical proposals.*

Similar remarks apply.

It is clear from this that the key factor is militancy. If it can be reduced, then both unemployment and inflation can be brought down. If not, something *may* be achieved by policies which succeed in stimulating labour-using investment, but it remains uncertain whether such policies can be found, or whether their effects are likely to be very great. A third possibility, reducing 'frictional' unemployment by the type of measures advocated by monetarists, should also be remembered.

9 Can we get back to full employment?

We can get back to full employment if, when the government follows a macroeconomic policy which gradually reflates demand, the share of profits gradually· increases, labour-using investment is encouraged, some cyclical and all structural unemployment is gradually absorbed and, despite the rise in profits and fall in unemployment, wage increases remain moderate, that is, not much in excess of the average rate of growth of labour productivity. With present arrangements, the government cannot ensure this happy chain of events. The final link in it is missing, and cannot be forged by the government alone. Macroeconomic policy is inadequate, and still is even when combined with incomes policies of the kind we have tried in the past. Import restrictions will only make matters worse. It may be possible to reduce unemployment by enlarging the public sector, or by job-subsidies (or reductions in job-taxes) of various kinds, but whether this can be done is uncertain. It is quite possible that measures such as these actually increase unemployment when all their indirect effects are taken into account. It is, in any case, likely to be a costly and inefficient route to full employment, supposing it gets us there at all. So, as things are, the government is unable to deliver full employment.

If this conclusion is accepted, it follows that we must be prepared to make some changes in present arrangements if we want to get back to full employment, and they will probably have to be fairly radical, otherwise they would already have been tried. Practical men will be able to point out the objections to such changes, and especially the prime objection that they are simply unacceptable to some powerful group, or just 'not on.' They may be right—for the present. But needs must when the devil drives. Quite a few changes which were 'not on' have been on. We have devalued the pound, we have introduced floating exchange rates, the dollar price of gold has quintupled, real wages have been severely cut in a period of incomes policy, and unemployment has risen to around $1\frac{1}{2}$ millions without a Labour Government reflating the economy. What practical men would have predicted all these 15 years ago? It is therefore not naïve to look seriously at some of the more radical measures described in Chapter 7.

In the writer's opinion no measures will be successful unless they include some reform of our present system for fixing wages. That system has evolved over a long period, and has many virtues. It is also very complex. Its main defect that concerns us here is that it places wage negotiators, both employers and workers, in a position in which the outcome of the negotiations is accelerating wage and price inflation unless unemployment is unacceptably high and/or profits are very low—and so low as to result in inadequate labour-using investment.

However much individual employers or unions may regret this outcome, there is very little that they, as individuals, can do about it. The union leader's job is to press for wage increases, and if he holds back without the assurance that others will do likewise his members are likely to suffer. The employer's job is to keep his business going, and that requires reasonably good labour relations. It will seldom appear right for him to resist wage demands to the point of a strike. The government, as the biggest employer in the economy, cannot always be asking employees in the public sector to 'set an example,' which means lagging behind wage increases elsewhere in the economy. So the collective interest in price stability and low unemployment is not secured by the present system.

Labour's bargaining strength in individual negotiations is now so strong that it can only be held back under existing arrangements by high unemployment, low profits, and, possibly, rather rapid inflation. True, it can also be held back from time to time by the crisis measures known as 'incomes policies.' But these are essentially temporary, and have failed to replace the other sanctions. For unemployment *has* risen, profits *have* fallen and inflation is still very rapid by historical standards. The engine driving the flywheel is too powerful for the brake, and it is only the tremendous friction being generated which stops further acceleration of the wheel, but also risks destroying it.

Employers have shown willingness to reform the wage-fixing system. The set of proposals put forward in 1977 by the CBI was briefly outlined in Chapter 7. There seems little doubt that any government would welcome changes which looked as if they might reconcile full employment and price stability. The trade union movement showed its willingness in 1976 and 1977 to restrain money wage increases so as to moderate the then very high rate of inflation, even though this resulted in real wage cuts. However, with few exceptions, it does not publicly admit that the system of wage fixing needs radical reform, nor has it provided much in the way of constructive proposals in this direction. Exceptionally, Basnett, General Secretary of the General and Municipal Workers Union and Chairman of the TUC (December 4, 1977) has stated that reforms are needed in the system of wage fixing in the public sector, and has put forward proposals. But the TUC's *Economic Review* for 1978, which has a great many proposals to make about numerous aspects of economic policy, has nothing to say about the need for reform of the wage-fixing system. It states 'the need for an orderly return to free collective bargaining,' reminds the reader that 'the TUC has stated that it is not a party to the Government's 10 per cent policy,' and admits that 'the approach of securing very large increases (in pay) in order to make up ground lost over the past three years would be self-defeating.' That is virtually all it has to say about wages. It has a great deal to say about the need for reflation and a reduction in unemployment, but it does not seem publicly prepared to recognise that the main obstacle to securing these desirable things is our unreformed wage-fixing system.

It seems highly unlikely that any useful reforms can be made in that system unless and until trade union leaders believe they are necessary, and convince their members of this as well. That will probably not be easy. Perhaps it will not be possible until a lot more water has flowed under the bridge. We will probably not be able to get back to full employment until that happens.

10 A measure of the full employment rate of unemployment in the UK

By Robert A. Laslett

INTRODUCTION

While it cannot be the case that, in a normally functioning economy, full employment is attained only when the number of registered unemployed falls to zero, it is also fairly generally recognized that in Britain at the moment there is considerably less than full employment and that the published unemployment figures provide some indication of this. What I have tried to do in this chapter is to arrive at a single figure for the unemployment rate that might reasonably be taken as representing full employment. For this purpose we have to have a definition of full employment. In line with Chapter 2, it seems desirable to define it as being a state of the labour market similar to that prevailing in the period 1948–66, that is as one in which job seekers encounter a comparable degree of difficulty in finding a job acceptable to them.

It might seem as though this would imply that full employment could only be said to have been reached when the average duration of spells of unemployment was the same as it had been in 1948–66. A number of complications prevent this deduction however. First, the composition of the labour force is not by age, by sex or by skills the same as it was in that period, so the average duration of unemployment could easily have changed while individuals in any one class continued to experience the same duration. Second, the duration of unemployment may reflect the choices of the unemployed as well as the state of the labour market.

One way of looking at the distinction we are trying to draw is as being that between the effects on measured unemployment of changes in the demand for and supply of labour. The definition of full employment envisages demand conditions similar to those of the 50s and 60s. These conditions will produce different measured rates of unemployment if supply-side conditions have changed. Given this definition in terms of similar demand conditions, the attempt to identify changes in full employment becomes that of estimating the extent of supply side changes.

There are considerable hazards in trying to disentangle demand changes from supply changes, and some of the procedures used in this chapter are rather arbitrary. Changes in the amount of unemployment that people choose (a 'supply side' phenomenon) may be affected by conditions on the demand side of the market, with possibly perverse consequences for policy. An illustration of this might be that when the demand for labour is very high, and people know they have the pick of the jobs on offer, they may be induced to spend a long time out of work searching for the ideal one. The fact that registered unemployment was high would not in these circumstances be a good indication of the need to increase demand. The position at the moment is much more complex than this for there does seem to be a deficiency of demand for labour and at the same time it has been suggested that there have been supply changes as well.

The two things whose effects are taken to be on the supply side of the labour market are changes in unemployment benefit and in the characteristics of the labour force. The paper starts with a review of the 'Phillips Curve' relation between inflation and unemployment, and goes on to discuss the possible consequences of changes in benefits and in characteristics. Obvious omissions from the analysis are any mention of the effects of incomes policies, which may have systematically distorted the structure of wages in such a way as to have increased unemployment, and of legislation concerning security of employment which may have reduced employers' willingness to take on labour. In the case of incomes policy, the argument is that its effect has been to increase the relative wages of the low-paid, with the result that their employment decreases, and it becomes more worthwhile for employers to move skilled workers to unskilled jobs when business is slack. This change should be reflected in the altering characteristics of the unemployed noted below. The argument about legislation on security is that the increased difficulty of shedding labour would discourage employers from hiring it in a boom that they did not expect to last. It is presumably mirrored by the delayed discharge of labour into unemployment in the slump, and it can be argued that the main effect will be to stabilise employment over the business cycle. But because the UK legislation was introduced at the bottom of a depression only the effect on hiring has been operating, with adverse effects on unemployment.

THE PHILLIPS CURVE

This originated in the observation that if the series for registered unemployment and for the rate of change of money wages were plotted against one another, the data for the UK presented a distinct pattern. Phillips in his original article (Phillips 1958) made use of data up to 1957, and found that a curve fitted to the years 1861–1913 roughly corresponded to the unemployment and inflation experience of both 1913–48 and 1948–57. Thus the first noteworthy feature of the pattern is its stability over a long period of time. The second, and the crucial one for the use of the curve in theory and in policy, is its downward slope.

The observation of such a stable relationship was taken as evidence of the possibility of making a 'tradeoff' between the two undesirables by policy means. It seemed to be possible to choose between worlds with a lot of inflation and rather little unemployment, or with little inflation and a lot of unemployment. In the late 1960s the pattern began to change its shape, however, and assumed the appearance of a random scatter. More recently there appears to have been an upward slope to the curve, with both unemployment and inflation increasing at the same time. (see for example McCracken *et al.* (1977), chart 16).

It is still feasible to believe that the Phillips relation persists, and has merely been concealed by other overlaying factors. This is the hypothesis of the shifted curve, and would mean that, without the influence of these other things, higher unemployment would still produce slower inflation. What, then, might be the other things that shifted the curve?

One prevalent idea has been that labour markets are affected by expectations of inflation. This may come about either from the supply side, with trades unions formulating their claims on the basis of comparability with what they observe or expect other unions to obtain, or from the demand side, as employers work out how much they will have to offer with reference to what they expect other employers to offer in competition. In extreme versions of this theory when unemployment is constant the rate of inflation is taken to equal the expected future rate of change of wages or prices. Any change in this expected rate will be reflected in an equal change in the actual inflation rate, as long as unemployment remains the same. In this view the Phillips curve has shifted because people have come to anticipate higher rates of inflation.

The expected rate of inflation is not however an ordinary macro-economic variable. For one thing it is not derivable from normal statistical sources, and is thus unlikely to be on a strictly comparable basis to other quantities. And while a survey could reveal the expectations of individuals and organisations, it is not clear whether their presumably differing opinions can be aggregated to give a satisfactory summary measure of what the economy as a whole expects. In the absence of such surveys the tendency has been to impose rather rigid schemes of expectation formation, and the doubt remains whether the evidence derived from testing such models bears upon the inflationary process or the imposed pattern of expectations.

But it seems highly likely that current inflation in prices does have an effect on wage settlements, presumably through the mechanism of expectations, while wage inflation in turn has an important effect on prices, as wages are a large component of costs. A change in expectations of inflation, either arising spontaneously or deriving from a change in prices, will therefore change the rate of wage increase associated with a given level of unemployment. In particular, a rise in the expected rate of inflation will increase the rate of wage increase at each level of unemployment, and the Phillips curve will shift outwards and upwards.

An alternative explanation of the shift in the Phillips curve is that of change in the nature of the labour market already mentioned in the introduction. If supply-side changes alter the level of unemployment associated with every level of demand, and if demand determines inflation, then they alter the unemployment/inflation relation. Specifically, an outward shift of the curve suggests that the level of unemployment associated with each level of demand has increased.

This is the line of approach with which this paper will be principally concerned, and is the one from which we will attempt to find out what level of unemployment in 1976 would correspond to full employment as experienced in the early 1960s.

UNEMPLOYMENT BENEFIT

It is now commonly suggested that changing the rate of unemployment benefit entitlement changes the level of unemployment itself, a phenomenon known as induced employment. A possible model of this process is that unemployed job-seekers will decide to spend longer looking for work the better their material circumstances while they are doing so. Such unemployment is clearly less pernicious than the predicament of men persistently unable to find work, firstly because it is to some extent the choice of the individual concerned, and second because it will help to increase the efficiency of the labour market in allocating people to the right jobs.

This suggests that the effect of increased unemployment benefits will be to reduce labour turnover by allowing better matching of people to jobs and encouraging more permanent attachments. On the other hand the increased benefits will tend to increase turnover in at least two ways. The first, that workers will be induced to quit by the generosity of the dole, seems unlikely to be of much importance for there are still plenty of drawbacks (eg loss of status and privacy, uncertainty about the future) associated with unemployment. The second is that workers will be happier about taking jobs in sectors of the economy where risks of unemployment are relatively high, and that employers will correspondingly find it profitable to expand in such areas. The net effect of increasing benefits is taken to be that it increases unemployment.

It seems, on the face of it, as though the considerable rise in unemployment benefit entitlement rates since the early 1960s would have had some effect on the level of unemployment in this country via this mechanism. In Table 10.1 are produced figures of the percentage ratio of benefit entitlements to earnings for a married couple with two children, and with the average earnings of an adult male manual worker, for the years 1948 to 1976. This benefit to earnings ratio is also called the 'replacement ratio'.

TABLE 10.1

The replacement ratio 1948–76

(percentages)

Year	(a)	(b)
1948	39.6	
1949	38.3	
1950	36.5	
1951	36.0	
1952	41.5	
1953	39.3	
1954	36.7	
1955	39.4	
1956	37.1	
1957	35.5	
1958	44.0	
1959	41.9	
1960	39.5	
1961	44.3	
1962	43.0	
1963	47.4	
1964	44.6	
1965	49.3	
1966	48.0	68.6
1967	51.8	73.2
1968	50.6	72.8
1969	47.6	71.0
1970	48.3	72.7
1971	51.8	77.9
1972	50.4	73.7
1973	49.5	70.6
1974	50.2	70.3
1975	48.3	67.0
1976	48.4	67.3

NOTE: (a) is (standard rate of unemployment benefit plus family allowances) expressed as a percentage of (earnings net of income tax, national insurance contributions and family allowances);

(b) is (a) plus (earnings related supplement) as a percentage of (net income).

N.B. Earnings related supplement was introduced in October 1966.

(1) *Earnings related supplement (ERS)*

One piece of circumstantial evidence in favour of the induced unemployment theory is the very rapid rise in 1966, coinciding exactly with the introduction of ERS. Looking at the distribution of the unemployed by their period out of work, however, this view becomes untenable, for the way in which the effect occurs is more like a sudden burst of sackings (a shake-out of the labour force) than a lengthening of search by the unemployed.

Maki and Spindler (1975) looked at the effects of ERS in the context of econometric estimates of the impact of unemployment compensation on the level of unemployment. They found that ERS alone seemed to have induced increased unemployment equal to 0.6 per cent of the work-force on average in the period 1967–72. Applying their estimates to the unemployment and benefits of 1976 produces a figure for ERS-induced unemployment of 1 per cent at that date. This figure would suggest that ERS alone had a very considerable influence on aggregate unemployment. There are, however, a number of difficulties with their analysis.

Firstly, the uptake of ERS was surprisingly slight, especially at first, and this is reflected in the much slighter rise in benefits actually paid than in the entitlements given in the table above. Their figures for the unemployment induced by ERS exceed the numbers actually receiving that benefit, except in 1970, and perhaps in the last three years, when there have been substantial increases in the numbers receiving ERS.

Secondly, one would expect a special benefit such as ERS to increase the proportion of claimants in the range of durations at which it is payable. This is not to be observed to any great extent with ERS, the relevant duration being two to twentysix weeks. To the extent to which it did occur, it was rather more marked among women, who generally did not qualify for the benefit, than among men.

Moreover Cubbin and Foley (1977) have shown that the use of the replacement ratio in their estimated equations does not allow unemployment to be predicted particularly well, and that much better results can be obtained with a 'permanent income' variable. They suggest that this shows the effects of increased income and wealth on people's desire for the things that unemployment provides, namely leisure and the chance to search the labour market more thoroughly.

Two other estimates of the unemployment induced by ERS are made by a working party set up by the Department of Employment (October 1976), and are both in the nature of maximal figures. The number of claimants of ERS at any one time did not exceed 100,000 in the period 1966–70, so even if it is assumed that all were induced to double their period out of work, the aggr₎gate unemployment total would only have increased by about 50,000, or 0.2 per cent of the 1970 work-force. Similarly the number of claimants in the two to twentysix weeks duration group increased by about 60,000 from 160,000 in 1962–3 to 220,000 in 1967–8, which were similar points in the business cycle. Again, if all of this change is attributed to the effect of ERS, its impact was no greater than 0.25 per cent of the work-force.

Exactly analogous points can be made for the redundancy grants introduced in the same period, for which the Department of Employment Working Party estimated a maximum effect on unemployment of 20,000 or 0.1 per cent of the 1970 work-force.

It is probably more realistic to take the Working Party's figures for the amount of unemployment induced by ERS, and to attribute a good deal of Maki and Spindler's correlation to the coincidence of the introduction of this particular benefit with an increase in unemployment which had other predominant causes. This is not to dismiss induced unemployment as a potentially important phenomenon, as the following section will show.

(2) *Taxation*

The replacement ratios presented in the table above use average earnings (net of income tax) as their denominator. This may not be a correct procedure, in view of the fact that unemployment is predominantly experienced by those with less-than-average earnings. Thus the general level of relevant replacement ratios may be considerably higher than those figures suggest. Moreover they may misstate the development of the replacement ratio over time. This could arise both because the tax threshold has been falling through the income distribution (from the 43rd percentile in 1959 to the 18th in 1974 according to the Survey of Personal Incomes, or from the 55th to the 32nd according to the Blue Book, see Diamond (1977), Table D8 p. 243 and Table D4 p. 239, and Board of Inland Revenue (1974)), and because the first rate of income tax has risen (from 6.8 per cent to 33 per cent over the same period), while the rate of income tax at average earnings has remained relatively static.

Because tax is deducted from the denominator of the expression for the replacement ratio, any increase in tax payments among those at risk of unemployment will increase the relevant replacement ratio. To find the true ratio for those at risk of unemployment, it would be necessary to find the ratio for each income level, and construct a weighted average of these figures. The appropriate weightings would be the proportions of the population at risk at each income level, but the information to construct such a set of weightings does not exist for the UK economy. Given below are the ratios for four points on the income distribution, and a weighted average based on the simplifying assumption that the population at risk of unemployment is uniformly spread between the median and the lower quartile of the income distribution. It should be noted that these series refer to standard benefit entitlement alone; ERS is not included.

These figures give some idea of the replacement ratios that apply at the margin at various earnings levels. This is to say that they properly apply only to the first week spent out of work. This can be illustrated for column (3), which is calculated on the basis that the individual involved would just earn enough in a full year's employment to be paying income tax. If he were to spend one week of the year without employment, his year's income would fall below the tax threshold, and all his tax payments would be refunded to him. If he spends another week unemployed, there are no further refunds to be made, and the replacement ratio he faces falls to that given in column (2).

Away from the tax threshold the meaning of the figures is rather more subtle. The earnings in all the columns are those that would accrue in a full year of employment: they are ex-ante or anticipated incomes. Actual incomes are by definition ex-post or realised, and may be composed both of earnings and benefit receipts. Men with different ex-ante incomes may have the same ex-post income if they suffer different periods of unemployment during the year, and will thus have different replacement ratios, since the ratio compares benefits with earnings foregone. The figures given in the table are for just one of these ratios, namely the one for men whose ex-ante earnings would just have brought them to the lower quartile, the tax threshold and the median respectively.

TABLE 10.2

Replacement ratios at various earnings levels, 1961/2 to 1975/6

(percentages)

Year	(1) Lower Quartile	(2) Below Tax Threshold	(3) Above Tax Threshold	(4) Median	(5) Weighted Average
1961/2	102.4	58.6	62.7	58.3	77.7
1962/3	102.3	58.6	62.7	57.1	76.5
1963/4	115.8	54.7	64.5	60.2	88.0
1964/5	111.9	54.7	64.5	57.1	84.5
1965/6	116.2	62.1	73.3	73.0	89.5
1966/7	100.2	62.1	73.3	67.7	79.2
1967/8	106.1	69.5	82.0	78.9	84.8
1968/9	101.4	76.4	90.2	75.4	85.4
1969/70	95.2	72.5	94.2	69.5	82.5
1970/71	99.0	69.3	99.1	79.4	86.5
1971/2	107.4	73.9	108.6	87.0	93.4
1972/3	104.8	70.4	114.9	95.8	94.3
1973/4	102.5	77.0	110.0	79.1	92.7
1974/5	97.2	77.6	115.8	78.4	93.1
1975/6		83.1	127.8		

Notes

(a) The Replacement Ratio is the standard rate of benefit entitlement including family allowances for a married couple with two children, expressed as a percentage of earnings.

(b) Years are fiscal years, except for the denominators in columns (1) and (4) in the years up to and including 1967, which are derived from income distributions for the earlier calendar year.

(c) Column (3) is $(1/1 - t)$ times column (2), where t is the effective first rate of income tax.

(d) Column (5) is calculated as

$$\frac{(\text{Column (1)} + \text{Column (2)}) \times (P - 25) + (\text{Column (3)} + \text{Column (4)}) \times (50 - P)}{50}$$

where P is the percentile at which the tax threshold falls in the income distribution. In 1963/4 and 1964/5 the tax threshold fell above the median. In 1967/8 and 1968/9 a second rate began below the median, and is included in the weighted average.

SOURCES: Diamond Commission 1977, Table D4, page 239.
Reports of the Commissioners of Inland Revenue.

These figures reveal two rather worrying things. The first is that an increasing proportion of the workforce seems in recent years to have been facing replacement ratios over 100 per cent, or a financial incentive to spend a part of the year out of work. They also reveal considerable injustices and inefficiencies inherent in the benefit system, arising because of a failure to keep tax thresholds significantly above the range of incomes of people seriously at risk of being unemployed. In particular, the increasingly radical change in marginal replacement ratios as income from employment passes the tax threshold (seen in the widening gap between the figures above and below the threshold in the table) cannot possibly reflect reasonable ideas about how compensation ought to be arranged.

Two lines of approach to this problem seem possible, and should be seriously considered by any government concerned with unemployment and the labour market. The first would be to raise the tax thresholds sufficiently to bring them out of the range of incomes where there are significant risks of unemployment. If the tax threshold was to be restored to the level of median income (where it stood on average in 1963–66), the tax exemption limit for a married couple ought to have stood in 1974–5 at over £1900. It should be correspondingly higher now because of wage increases since that date, but in autumn 1977 was only £1455. An alternative scheme would be to restore the reduced-rate bands of income tax, and thus make the effect of the onset of income tax less severe, and the Budget of April 1978 was a step in this direction. The first rate of income tax in 1963–6 was nominally 20 per cent, and actually only 15.6 per cent because of earned income relief.

The second approach would be to reduce the replacement ratio for those above the income tax threshold to correspond with the ratio for those below. If a fixed benefit level is to be retained, the obvious way of doing this would be to make benefits liable for income tax. With the current system of collecting income tax by withholding it from each week's pay, and refunding past tax payments to those who become unemployed, the mechanics of taxing benefits would be that refunds would be reduced rather than that deduction would be made from benefit income. Nonetheless, this measure would probably be both administratively difficult and exceedingly unpopular for imposing a loss of income on those who, while paying income tax, are not particularly well off. It might be decided that the implied replacement ratios above the threshold were too low, and this could be corrected by a deliberate decision to increase benefits or to raise the tax threshold as suggested above.

An incidental advantage of this system would be that it would reduce horizontal inequality among those with the same income who become unemployed at different times of the year. At present the conditions enjoyed by tax payers who become unemployed are less generous at the beginning of the tax year than they are at the end, for the period over which tax refunds are available depends on tax paid in the current year and thus on the time elapsed of that year. The reduction of refunds would partially eliminate this effect.

On balance, the taxation of existing benefits is deflationary, while raising the tax threshold or lowering the first rate are expansionary. Some combination of the two is probably desirable, especially if we believe that the present fiscal stance of government is correct.

THE CHARACTERISTICS OF THE UNEMPLOYED

The data in this section are taken from the sample surveys of the unemployed taken in 1961, 1964, 1973 and 1976, in which the unemployed population are analysed by some at least of the characteristics that might affect their chances of getting a job.

Two caveats should be made before we proceed to a comparison of the surveys themselves. The first is that there are differences in definition between the surveys, the most serious being that the 1961 figures exclude registered unemployed who were not claiming benefit. The second is that there is not sufficient variety among the cyclical phases represented by the surveys to be confident in separating cyclical from structural changes. Only the 1976 survey refers to a date at which the labour market was markedly slack by comparison with preceding or succeeding years.

Table 10.3 gives the survey results on the prospects of the unemployed, with some breakdown of the poor prospects category by their characteristics.

The effect that I have tried to isolate from these figures may be called the composition effect, and is the extent to which unemployment has increased because of changes in the composition

TABLE 10.3

Analysis of the unemployed by their prospects of obtaining work

Prospects	1961 Thousand	1961 %	1964 Thousand	1964 %	1973 Thousand	1973 %	1976 Thousand	1976 %
Good	46.2	19.5	72.5	23.2	134.2	25.7	316.0	28.1
Limited by local opportunities	35.8	16.3	54.0	17.3	68.8	13.2	268.9	23.9
Poor	140.6	64.2	186.4	59.6	319.9	61.1	539.3	48.0
Poor, due to								
(a) Age	34.0	15.5	63.2	20.2	71.7	13.7	67.2	6.0
(b) Physical Condition	48.6	22.2	60.0	19.2	81.6	15.6	100.1	8.9
(c) Lack of Enthusiasm	19.0	8.7	29.3	9.4	71.2	13.6	119.4	10.6
(d) Other	39.0	17.8	33.9	10.8	95.4	18.2	252.6	22.5
Total	219.0	100.0	312.9	100.0	522.9	100.0	1124.2	100.0

The numbers in each category are estimates derived from the samples on the assumption that the structure of the unemployed who were surveyed was exactly the same as that of the whole population of unemployed. Figures include both male and female and refer to the U.K.

SOURCES: Department of Employment Gazette April 1962 pp. 131–7, April 1966 pp. 156–7, March 1974 pp. 211–21, June 1977 pp. 559–74.

of the labour force that is offering itself for employment by registering at job centres. As usual a major problem in isolating one
effect is the interaction of supply and demand, in this case because
changes in employers' requirements also affect the characteristics
of the recorded unemployment.

In order to extract any information from a comparison of the
surveys, it must first be assumed that the meanings of the descrip-
tions of prospects did not change from one survey to the next.
One reason to suspect that there might have been such changes
is that it is possible for Employment Officers to be rather more
objective about some of the characteristics, for instance physical
disability or old age, than about others, notably enthusiasm for
work. Another and more important reason is that allocation into
the poor prospects category is not likely to be fully independent
of the current state of demand.

A second necessary assumption is that Employment Officers are
by and large correct in the prospects that they assign. If so,
we would expect that those whose characteristics lead them to
be classified as poor prospects when they come onto the unemployment register will at all times form a larger proportion of the
unemployed than they do of the employed population. Thus though
the poor prospects are likely to be among the first to lose their
jobs in a downswing of demand, the preponderance of the good
prospects among the employed will eventually show through in
discharges as the downswing continues. Deep recession will be
accompanied by a relatively high proportion of good prospects
on the register, and a relatively low proportion of poor prospects,
in comparison to more normal times.

Looking at the proportions for 1976 relative to those of the
other years, we see that this has indeed happened. For example
the physically handicapped have decreased as a proportion of
the unemployed, while the absolute number unemployed for this
reason have increased, and increased far faster than it is possible
to believe the handicapped have in the population as a whole.
The implication is that many, perhaps disproportionately many,
handicapped workers have lost their jobs in the recent slump,
but that the effect of this on the statistics is modified by the
fact that disproportionately few were employed in the first place.
Correspondingly the proportion of poor prospects, and of most
of its component categories, has decreased. At the same time
the absolute numbers in all of the categories except the aged

increased after 1973. In what follows, changes in the numbers with prospects that are good, or limited by local opportunities, are taken to represent unemployment arising from slack demand in the labour market, and attention is concentrated on the poor prospects as the measure of changes on the supply side.

The most extreme assumption one could make about the composition effect would be that all the poor prospects in the population are unemployed at all times, and that any increase in their numbers over time represents an increase in the irreducible minimum level of unemployed. On this assumption the maximum impact between 1964 and 1976 would be of the order of 350,000 or about 1.5 per cent of the 1976 working population.

This construction is untenable, both because the poor prospects are by no means unemployable, and because some of the categories that it comprises are themselves not independent of the level of economic activity. Most clearly this may be the case with the unenthusiastic; prolonged unemployment and poor local opportunities may combine to reduce people's enthusiasm for work. Equally, the Employment Officers' assessments of an individual's chance of finding employment are presumably not independent of the state of the labour market. A person whose skills and availability make him a poor prospect when the labour market is slack could easily be recorded as a good prospect when the market is relatively tight. If this effect occurred, the fact that the samples other than 1976 were taken in relatively good years would tend to decrease the proportion of poor prospects recorded in those years in relation to those of 1976, and exaggerate the recent increase in their numbers.

Turning now to the 'Other' category, a more detailed breakdown forces us to revise the maximal estimate of the effect of compositional change of the unemployment figures. This breakdown is available only for the last two. These figures are given in Table 10.4.

The increase in the proportion of the unskilled could be either a compositional or a cyclical effect. The declining proportion in group (ii) suggests a phenomenon similar to that of the physically handicapped. But much the most important group is that seeking short-term work only, as large in 1976 as the numbers of poor prospects due to physical disability or lack of enthusiasm.

One hypothesis that might cover the facts is that of the dual labour market, divided into 'regular' and 'casual' segments. On this theory, the recent increase in unemployment is partly a result

TABLE 10.4

Composition of category (d) of poor prospects of Table 10.3

	Reason for inclusion in the category	1973		1976	
		Thousands	%	Thousands	%
(i)	Experience or skill not acceptable to employers	6.5	1.2	21.5	1.9
(ii)	Personality problems	10.1	1.9	15.1	1.3
(iii)	'Probably unable to hold down a job'	20.6	3.9	49.9	4.4
(iv)	Seeks short-term work only	38.7	7.4	116.7	10.4
(v)	Other	19.6	3.7	49.2	4.4
	Total	95.4	18.2	252.6	22.5

Notes of sources as Table 10.3.
Note to table 10.4: Due to rounding errors, the figures given in the columns do not add exactly to the figures given as totals.

of changes in the registration habits of the workless. Partly because it has become financially more rewarding (see the section on unemployment benefit above) and partly because of changes in attitudes towards those who admit to being unemployed, men and women from the casual segment who would previously have left the work-

TABLE 10.5

Analysis by sex of the unemployed seeking short-term work

	1964		1973		1976	
	Thousands	%	Thousands	%	Thousands	%
Men	1.2	0.5	30.5	6.8	94.1	10.7
Women	8.1	10.7	8.2	10.9	22.6	9.2
Total	9.3	3.0	38.7	7.4	116.7	10.4

Notes and sources: as Table 10.3. Notes to table 10.5 (i) The percentages given in the first two rows refer to total numbers unemployed of each sex.
(ii) The 1964 figures are not fully comparable with the later ones, and should be taken as indicative only.

force altogether when they did not have a job now remain in it by registering their unemployment. It has sometimes been suggested that more women than men would be involved in this as they are more likely to be in the casual segment, but a breakdown of category (iv) of Table 10.4 does not reveal this. On the contrary, the increase has been very much more marked among men than among women. Even the previous tendency for a greater proportion of the female unemployed to be registered for short-term work only was reversed in 1976.

It seems that the recent increase in the number and proportions of the unemployed seeking short-term work only must reflect a supply-side change in the labour market, and has thus to some degree changed the meaning of the unemployment figures. As usual, however, it is impossible to be sure of the extent to which it results from increases in overall unemployment.

THE FULL EMPLOYMENT RATE OF UNEMPLOYMENT

The aim of this section is to suggest what rate of unemployment in 1976 would have corresponded to full employment as understood in before 1966. The technique used here is to make allowance for the unemployment induced by ERS, and for that due to composition effects, and to add these allowances to the full employment rate of the 1948/66 period. The average rate of unemployment in that period was 1.7 per cent, falling to 1.5 per cent in the high activity years 1961 and 1966 and lower still in 1951 and 1955. An average rate is used as the base level because these high activity rates were clearly unstable even in the conditions of the period. Some allowance must also be made for the extent to which induced unemployment and the composition effect overlap, and the calculations proceed on the assumption that just as large a proportion of compositional as of other unemployment is induced. A double counting correction is subtracted.

As an example of the sort of calculation involved, one might take Maki and Spindler's estimate of induced unemployment, together with the entire increase in the numbers of poor prospects, as an outside estimate of compositional change. The former adds 1 per cent of the 1976 workforce, the latter 1.5 per cent to the full employment rate. After making the double counting correction, we add these to the 1.7 per cent base rate, and the full employment rate emerges as 3.8 per cent. We have already suggested that both components of this figure are likely to be very much on the high side, but it is of some interest to note that even this set of figures does not explain the 1976 rate of 5.9 per cent.

In the attempt to derive a more reasonable figure for the unemployment induced by ERS, we proceed on a basis analogous to that used by the Department of Employment. At the end of 1975 there were 235,000 people receiving ERS. If each of them was being induced by the benefit to spend twice as long on the register as he or she would have done in its absence, the additional unemployment generated would have been 117,500 or 0.5 per cent of the workforce (redundancy grants add a further 0.1 per cent on the basis that their proportionate effect has not increased since 1970). It is also necessary to take a more cautious view of how changes in the prospects of the unemployed relate to changes in the available supply of labour. If we take the entire change in the numbers seeking short-term work as a change in either the nature of the labour supply or of the meaning of the unemployment figures, we have an increase of 108,000 or 0.45 per cent of the 1976 work-force between 1964 and 1976. Similarly the change attributable to an increase in the number unenthusiastic for work is 90,000, or 0.38 per cent. Both of these might be accepted as being at least in part changes in the supply of labour as usually conceived of, a conclusion that is not necessarily applicable to the remaining categories of the poor prospects group. Of these remaining categories I am inclined to accept only the increase in the number with unacceptable skills as a supply-side difficulty, though the phenomenon might equally arise out of changes in the pattern of skills demanded by employers. The final difficulty is one that has already been mentioned, that enthusiasm for work may well decrease with prolonged unemployment and demoralisation. This could be included in the calculations on an ad hoc basis, but it seems better simply to bear this in mind when interpreting the figures.

A summary of the modifications to be made is as follows:

	Number	Percentage
Average unemployment 1948/66		1.70
1964–76 increase due to:		
Numbers seeking short-term work only	108,000	0.45
Numbers lacking enthusiasm for work	90,000	0.38
Numbers lacking suitable skills. (Half of the change between 1964 and 1976)	80,000	0.03
Total Composition Effect Increase	206,000	0.86
Effect of ERS	117,500	0.49
Effect of redundancy grants	23,900	0.10
Total allowance for induced unemployment	141,400	0.59
Double Counting Correction	−38,100	−0.16
1976 'Full Employment Rate'		2.99

A similar calculation for 1973 yields a full-employment rate of 2.3 per cent, about 0.6 per cent above the 1948–66 average. 1973 was a year of relatively high activity compared with 1976, and these estimates can be taken as an indication of the peak and trough of the cycle. It would be useful to have a figure for full employment at the midpoint of the cycle, and an obvious way of approximating this is to average the 1973 and 1976 figures, giving a result of 2.6 per cent, about 1 per cent above the 1948–66 average. Unfortunately this procedure imposes a number of assumptions: (1) That 1973 and '76 were respectively peak and trough. Doubts attach particularly to the latter, for the peak of unemployment was not reached until September 1977. (2) That all compositional and induced changes unrelated to demand occurred before 1973. This is implied by taking all change between '73 and '76 to be cyclical, or demand linked. (3) That the cyclical peak and trough were comparable deviations from the trend of activity, and that the full employment rate varies linearly with such deviations from trend. For these reasons it is likely that the actual mid-point measure of full employment unemployment rather exceeds the simple average of the 1973 and '76 figures.

The figures for unemployment given in this chapter do not (in line with official figures) include adult students, whereas those in Scott's chapters do include them. The average number of students registered as unemployed in 1973 was 11,500 (0.04 per cent of the workforce) and in 1976 was 58,000 (0.24 per cent). It is not clear what difference this should make. By definition students are seeking short term work only, and this would suggest that they should be added to the composition effect in their entirety. This would mean however that we were prepared to accept, as a description of full employment, a state in which it is no easier to get a summer job than it was in 1976, which may well be a prejudicial implication in terms of work experience. And because the student body is not homogeneous with the rest of the labour force, a simple addition of the two would tend to confuse offsetting changes in both categories with no change in either. Bearing this in mind the addition of the student unemployed to the full employment rate gives figures of 2.32 per cent in 1973 and of 3.23 per cent in 1976.

In conclusion, it will be noted that no attempt has yet been made to estimate the effect on unemployment rates of the tax-induced increase in replacement ratios. This is partly because the uncertainty of the figures makes any estimate rather unreliable, and for this reason a conjectural calculation will be used to supply the deficiency. The mean of the weighted-average replacement ratios (Column (5) of Table 10.2) over the years 1961–2 to 1966–7 is 82.5, while in the years 1971–2 to 1974–5 it is 93.5. This represents an increase of 13 per cent. If the elasticity of the full employment rate of unemployment with respect to the replacement ratio was unity, there would also have been a 13 per cent increase in that rate, taking it from 1.7 per cent in 1948–66 to 1.9 per cent in 1971–5.

(In this context it is of some interest to note that, in their 1976 survey, the Department of Employment found that 3.4 per cent of their sample of the unemployed were unenthusiastic for work on the grounds that their prospective wage was unlikely to exceed their income when unemployed. This would gross up to 30,200 people in the unemployed population as a whole, or 0.13 per cent of the workforce, which provides some confirmation of the suggested order of magnitude of the effect.)

This is hardly a dramatic change, and does not seriously affect the validity of the foregoing calculations. The possibility remains however that the elasticity is higher than this, particularly in the long term as the implications of the replacement ratio are worked out. And it is equally possible that important behavioural changes occur as the replacement ratio reaches 100 per cent. While these issues are conceptually interesting, I do not myself believe that they go very far towards explaining the present rate of unemployment in this country. The tax and benefit systems may be in need of reform, but it would be a mistake to believe that reforms of these systems alone would help us very much in getting back to full employment.

Endnotes

4. INFLATION AND WAGE RESTRAINT

1. These and subsequent estimates in this paragraph are from Brown and Browne, 1968, Appendix 3, for the years 1923–38 and 1948–60. For the years 1960–66 index numbers with a similar coverage from *British Labour Statistics Historical Abstract 1886–1968*, Table 52, were linked on. The industries included are (broadly) manufacturing, mining and quarrying, construction, gas, electricity and water, transport and communication, certain services and public administration. Average rates of increase were found by fitting exponential curves to the data.

2. See Scott, June 1977, p. 234 for a table summarising estimates of the yield gap from 1926 to 1974.

5. LABOUR-SAVING VERSUS LABOUR-USING INVESTMENT

1. See, for example, McCracken et. al., June 1977, p. 157 et. seq.; Flemming 1976 and New Year 1977; Gruen, 1977.

2. The author has attempted this elsewhere (Scott, November 1976).

3. Rates of return here, and in what follows, are all calculated with respect to a 'no-change' alternative (i.e. no change in quantities—relative prices are allowed to change). There is no space to justify this procedure here, but it must be admitted that the resulting rates of return are not those which

are strictly relevant to profit maximisation decisions, and hence they need not be equalised at the margin. The writer does not believe that this is a serious objection.

4. If wages increase at a constant proportionate rate, this should not be a straight line, but curving upwards. However, in what follows we have, for simplicity, assumed a linear increase.

5. If wages increase at a constant proportionate rate during the life of the enterprise, WQ will not be a straight line (as shown) but will curve upwards. B and C will therefore not be parallelograms (as shown) but will become fatter as time passes. They will therefore tend to fall *more* than proportionately when T is reduced. Hence a shortening in life will tend to (slightly) favour labour-using investment.

6. For each of the seven industrial subdivisions in Table 5.2, we calculated the difference in the exponential rates of growth of male and female employment between 1959 and 1966 (1959 was chosen as being the earliest year for which directly comparable employment estimates were available in the *Department of Employment Gazette*, October 1975). We then calculated what male and female employment would have been in each industry in 1974 if (a) total employment in the industry had changed between 1966 and 1974 in the way it actually did, and (b) the same *difference* in growth rates had persisted. We compared these hypothetical employment figures with the actual ones, and took the difference between them as measuring the extent to which male and female employment changes were *not* explained by changes in the structure of industry. We thus calculated that, for males, 85 per cent of the actual fall of 1.18 millions in employment from 1966 to 1974 could be explained by changes in the structure of industry; whereas for females, 76 per cent of the actual increase of 0.72 millions in employment from 1966 to 1974 could be explained in this way. Had we used a finer breakdown of industry, with more than 7 groups, these percentages would probably have been still larger.

7. The paper argued 'that the effective margin for expansion of industrial output might be considerably smaller than that suggested by conventional statistics. This was because not all industries had the same amount of spare capacity. In addition, shortages of certain types of labour, materials and components could preclude any substantial increases in output. Some of the scheduled spare capacity might in fact be machinery for whose products there would never be customers, either because they could not be priced competitively or because their design, quality, marketing or delivery dates were not competitive .... Examples given by Sir Ronald (McIntosh, Director General of NEDO) of specific industrial problems included imports accounting for 40 per cent of the UK market in fractional horsepower motors even though there was 30 per cent spare capacity among UK manufacturers'. (*Financial Times*, Oct. 11, 1977, p. 40.)

7. POLICIES TO RESTORE FULL EMPLOYMENT

1. In case some readers find this surprising, the following simplified arithmetical example may be helpful. Suppose the government increases expenditure by employing more people (who would otherwise be unemployed) in public services (education, health, public administration etc.) by £1 million per annum, and that the people concerned find their incomes increased by £0.6 millions, since they were receiving £0.4 millions before in social security benefits and since they must now pay more in direct taxation. Let them save £0.1 millions of this extra income and spend £0.5 million on personal consumption. Let the government levy £0.6 million extra net taxes on others, who cut their savings by £0.1 million and consumption by £0.5 million. Then the government borrowing requirement is unchanged, and, taking the rest of the economy as a whole, private savings and private consumption are unchanged. The only changes which have occurred so far are (a) the increase in public service employment and (b) the increase in tax rates. It is (b) which creates the difficulty mentioned in the text.

2. It may be asked why the measures lower private consumption and investment, when the arithmetical example of the previous footnote showed that they would be unchanged. However, the circumstances are now different, for we are assuming that total unemployment is only slightly reduced. Hence the extra workers in public services must come mainly from the marketed sector, and total private sector demand must be cut. If, for example, *all* the extra workers in the public sector came from the marketed sector, and cost £1 million per annum, and if they would also have earned this in the marketed sector, then it is likely that the value of private consumption and investment, at market prices, would have to be cut by rather more than £1 million, in view of the higher indirect taxes levied on private consumption which would be lost to the State.

Appendix:
Explanation of Table 5.1

The figures in Table 5.1 show rates of return on labour-using and labour-saving investment for different ratios of profits to value-added. In order to calculate them, we have made the following assumptions, all of which are chosen with a view to making the investments we are concerned with 'typical' for UK manufacturing industry.

When rates of return on both types of investment are the same, we assume that (i) the share of profits in value-added is 30 per cent, (ii) output grows at 3 per cent per annum, (iii) employment is stationary, (iv) investment is 20 per cent of value-added, (v) investment is equally divided between labour-using and labour-saving investment each of which has the characteristics described in the text (i.e., labour-using investment increases both output and employment, while labour-saving investment does not change output but cuts employment), (vi) the economic lives of both types of investment are the same, and are given by the length of time it would take for wages to grow sufficiently to equal the whole of value-added when the share of profits is as in (i) and when wage rates grow at 3 per cent per annum and employment and value-added are constant. The result of making these assumptions is that the rate of return on each type of investment works out at 10.9 per cent per annum, and the length of life is approximately 12 years. Labour-using investment leads to an increase of output of 3 per cent, accompanied by a rise in employment of approximately 1.3 per cent, whereas labour-saving investment has no effect on output and reduces employment by approximately 1.3 per cent. So the net result is a growth in output of 3 per cent and no change in total employment, as assumed.

Assumptions (i), (ii), (iii), and (iv) may be justified by reference to Tables 5.2 & 5.3 considering the period 1956–66, when the share of profits in manufacturing value-added was 31 per cent, output grew at 3.5 per cent per annum, employment at 0.5 per cent per annum, and investment (as conventionally defined) averaged 15.6 per cent of value-added. We have not taken these figures precisely, and, in particular, have assumed that a wider definition of investment (including all costs of change, such as some advertising and marketing expenses, research and development and part of management salaries) would lead to an appreciably higher share of gross investment. The assumption of zero growth in labour force which we have taken for simplicity requires a lower growth of output. We have assumed a rate of growth of real product-wage of 3 per cent per annum which is the same as the assumed rate of productivity growth. Assumption (v) is a very rough guess.

The other rates of return shown in the table have been found by varying the assumed ratio of profits to value-added. All other 'physical' quantities are kept constant, and the change in profits' share is thus assumed to be due to higher wage-rates. It is assumed that the rate of growth of real wage-rates is the same, 3 per cent per annum, although in the long-run this must depend on the share of profits and the amount and composition of investment. However, the figures in the table can be regarded as rates of return which businessmen might calculate if they stuck to unchanged assumptions in this respect, as seems likely for a time at least.

List of References

Bacon, R. and Eltis, W. *Britain's Economic Problem: Too Few Producers*. 2nd. Ed. (London: Macmillan, 1978)

Ball, R. J., Burns, T. and Laury, J. S. E. 'The role of exchange rate changes in balance of payments adjustment: the United Kingdom Case', *The Economic Journal*, (March 1977)

Basnett, D. 'A way out of warfare over pay', *The Sunday Times*, (4 December 1977)

Beveridge, Sir William. *Full Employment in a Free Society*. (London: Allen & Unwin, 1944)

Board of Inland Revenue. *Inland Revenue Statistics 1974*. (HMSO 1974)

Brittan, S. *The Treasury under the Tories 1951–1964*, (Harmondsworth: Penguin Books, 1974)

Brittan, S. 'The Political Economy of British Union Monopoly', *Three Banks Review*, (Sept. 1976)

Brittan, S. and Lilley, P. *The Delusion of Incomes Policy* (London: Maurice Temple Smith, 1977)

Brown, E. H. Phelps with Browne, M. H. *A Century of Pay* (London: Macmillan, 1968)

Brown, E. H. Phelps, 'A Non-monetarist View of the Pay Explosion', *Three Banks Review*, (March 1975)

Cairncross, Sir Alec, Kay, J. A. and Silberston, A. 'The regeneration of manufacturing industry', *Midland Bank Review*, (Autumn 1977)

Cambridge Department of Applied Economics, *Economic Policy Review*. (February 1975, March 1976, March 1977, March 1978).

Confederation of British Industry, *The future of pay determination* (London: CBI, June 1977).

Corden, W. M., Little, I. M. D. and Scott, M. FG. *Import Controls versus Devaluation and Britain's Economic Prospects* (London: Trade Policy Research Centre, March 1975).

Cubbin, J. S. and Foley, K. 'The Extent of Benefit-Induced Unemployment in Great Britain: Some New Evidence', *Oxford Economic Papers*, (March 1977).

Department of Employment 'The changed relationship between unemployment and vacancies', *Department of Employment Gazette*, (October 1976).

Department of Employment Gazette, Sample surveys of the unemployed, issues for Apr. 1962 (pp. 131–7), April 1966 (pp. 156–7), March 1974 (pp. 211–21), June 1977 (pp. 559–74).

Diamond Commission. Royal Commission on the Distribution of Income and Wealth (Chairman: Lord Diamond). *Report No. 5, Third Report on the Standing Reference.* (London: HMSO, Cmnd. 6999, 1977).

Dow, J. C. R. and Dicks-Mireaux, L. A. 'The Excess Demand for Labour: A Study of Conditions in Great Britain, 1946–56', *Oxford Economic Papers*, (February 1958).

Employment Policy (London: HMSO, Cmd. 6527, May 1944).

Flemming, J. *Inflation* (Oxford: Oxford University Press, 1976).

Flemming, J. 'Adjust the Real Elements in a Changing Economy', in *Catch '76 . . . ?: 14 Escapes from Economic Derangement.* (London: Institute of Economic Affairs, Occasional Paper Special No. 47, February 1976).

Flemming, J. S., Price, L. D. D., Ingram, D. H. A., and Byers, Mrs. S. A., 'Trends in company profitability' and 'The cost of capital, finance and investment', *Bank of England Quarterly Bulletin*, (March and June 1976).

Flemming, J. 'The British Economy in 1977', *Financial Times*, (New Year, 1977).

Flemming, J. 'An Economist's View of Inflation', in *The Political Economy of Inflation*, ed. Hirsch, F. and Goldthorpe, J. H. (London: Martin Robertson, 1978).

Friedman, M. and Laidler, D. E. W. *Unemployment versus Inflation?: An Evaluation of the Phillips Curve (with a British Commentary)* (London: Institute of Economic Affairs, Occasional Paper 44, 1975).

Friedman, M. *Inflation and Unemployment: The New Dimension of Politics* (London: Institute of Economic Affairs, Occasional Paper 51, 1977).

Goldthorpe, J. H. 'The Current Inflation: Towards a Sociological Account', in *The Political Economy of Inflation*, ed. Hirsch, F. and Goldthorpe, J. H. (London: Martin Robertson, 1978).

Gruen, F. H. 'Structural Unemployment as a Rival Explanation—A Survey of an Inconclusive Argument', *Kiel Conference on Unemployment and Capital Shortage in the World Economy*, (June 1977).

Hartog, H den and Tjan, H. S. 'Investments, Wages, Prices and Demand for Labour (A Clay-Clay Vintage Model for the Netherlands),' *De Economist*, (1976).

Jay, P. *A General Hypothesis of Employment, Inflation and Politics* (London: Institute of Economic Affairs, Occasional paper 46, 1976).

Killingsworth, C. C. 'Structural Unemployment in the United States', in Stieber, J. (ed.), *Employment Problems of Automation and Advanced Technology* (London: Macmillan, 1966).

Laidler, D. E. W. and Parkin, J. M. 'Inflation—A Survey', *The Economic Journal*, (December 1975).

MacDougall, Sir Donald, 'Inflation in the United Kingdom', *The Economic Record*, (December 1959).

Maki, D. and Spindler, Z. A. 'The Effect of Unemployment Compensation on the Rate of Unemployment in Great Britain', *Oxford Economic Papers*, (November 1975).

Matthews, R. C. O. 'Why has Britain had Full Employment since the War?' *Economic Journal*, (September, 1968).

Matthews, R. C. O. and King, M. A. 'The British economy: problems and policies in the late 1970's, *Midland Bank Review*, (February 1977).

McCracken, P., Carli, G., Giersch, H., Karaosmanoglu, A., Komiya, R., Lindbeck, A., Marjolin, R. and Matthews, R. *Towards Full Employment and Price Stability* (Paris: OECD, June 1977).

Meade, J. E. *The Intelligent Radical's Guide to Economic Policy: The Mixed Economy*. (London: Allen and Unwin, 1975).

Minford, P. 'North Sea Oil and the British Economy', *The Banker*, (December 1977).

Nordhaus, W. D. 'The Political Business Cycle', *The Review of Economic Studies*, (April 1975).

Odling-Smee, J. and Hartley, N. *Some Effects of Exchange Rate Changes* (London: Government Economic Service Working Paper No. 2, March 1978).

Phelps, E. S. 'Money-Wage Dynamics and Labour-Market Equilibrium', *Journal of Political Economy*, (1968).

Phillips, A. W. 'The Relation Between Unemployment and the Rate of Change of Money Wages in the U.K. 1861–1957', *Economica*, (November 1958).

Scott, M. FG. 'Investment and Growth', *Oxford Economic Papers*, (November 1976).

Scott, M. FG. 'The Test Rate of Discount and Changes in Base-Level Income in the United Kingdom', *Economic Journal*, (June 1977).

Solow, R. M. 'The Nature and Sources of Unemployment in the United States', *Wicksell Lectures 1964*, (Uppsala: Almquist and Wicksell, 1964).

Solow, R. M. 'Macro-policy and Full Employment' in Ginzberg, E. (ed.), *Jobs for Americans* (Englewood Cliffs, 1976).

Taylor, C. T. 'Why is Britain in a recession?', *Bank of England Quarterly Bulletin*, (March 1978).

Tobin, J. 'Inflation and Unemployment', *American Economic Review*, (March 1972).

Trades Union Congress, *Economic Review 1978*, (1978).

Turvey, R. 'Structural change and structural unemployment', *International Labour Review*, (September–October 1977).

Index